Intra-Industry Trade

Also by Herbert G. Grubel

FORWARD EXCHANGE
THE INTERNATIONAL MONETARY SYSTEM

Also by P. J. Lloyd

NON-TARIFF DISTORTIONS OF AUSTRALIAN TRADE

INTRA-INDUSTRY TRADE

The Theory and Measurement of International Trade in Differentiated Products

HERBERT G. GRUBEL
Professor of Economics, Simon Fraser University

and

P. J. LLOYD
Senior Fellow, Australian National University

A HALSTED PRESS BOOK

JOHN WILEY & SONS
NEW YORK

First published 1975 *by*
THE MACMILLAN PRESS LTD

Published in the U.S.A.
by Halsted Press, a Division
of John Wiley & Sons, Inc.
New York.

Printed in Great Britain

Library of Congress Cataloging in Publication Data

Grubel, Herbert G
  Intra-industry trade.

  "A Halsted Press book."
  1. Commerce. 2. Commerce—Mathematical models.
3. Commercial policy. I. Lloyd, Peter J., joint
author. II. Title.
HF1007.G73   382   74–13576
ISBN 0–470–33000–7

Contents

List of Tables

List of Figures

Preface

This study began during 1969 when we were colleagues at the Department of Economics, Research School of Pacific Studies, Australian National University in Canberra, Australia. We discovered that we were both intrigued by the existence of what Balassa has called 'intra-industry trade', the simultaneous export and import of goods from the same industry. This general phenomenon had not been studied seriously and, consequently, we began a systematic effort to quantify its magnitude. The results of this work are presented in Part I of this book. They persuaded us that intra-industry trade is a phenomenon worth further theoretical and empirical analysis.

In Part II we present a number of models capable of explaining intra-industry trade. These models are based on the modification of several of the important simplifying assumptions of the traditional Heckscher–Ohlin model, such as zero transportation, storage and selling costs, the existence of perfect competition, and constant returns to scale. By far the most important results are produced by the introduction of the possibility that there are increasing returns to scale due to the savings from longer runs in the manufacture of differentiated products. In this part of the analysis we are able to draw together recent work on economies of scale and models of trade in differentiated products associated with the names of Daly, Linder, Drèze and Vernon. We close the book with several chapters considering the implications of the analysis for some basic theorems of trade theory, for economic policies and further empirical research.

A number of colleagues offered useful suggestions on parts of earlier drafts. We would like to thank particularly Heinz Arndt, Robert Baldwin, David Bensusan-Butt, Max Corden, Harry Johnson, Irving Kravis and other colleagues or former colleagues at the Australian National University, the University of Pennsylvania and the Simon Fraser University. We also express our gratitude to Mrs Audrey Cornish who calculated the measures of intra-industry trade for the OECD countries in Chapter 3 and for the EEC countries in Chapter 9. The Australian Government generously made available to us extremely dis-aggregated trade statistics on an electronic tape, which resulted in calculations summarised in Chapter 4. Without the generous supply of computer facilities and research assistance by the Australian National University this study would not have been possible. We thank especially Heinz Arndt for his support.

Vancouver, B.C., Canada   H.G.G.
Canberra, Australia   P.J.L.

1 Introduction

In this book we measure, explain and test empirically some aspects of international trade in differentiated products which are close substitutes. For convenience of expression and following a tradition to be outlined in the last part of this chapter, we refer to this phenomenon as 'intra-industry trade'.[1] This term describes aptly the international trade in differentiated products because commonly used statistical trade classification schemes result in much of this trade showing up as the simultaneous export and import of products belonging to the same 'industry', thus representing the exchange of goods and services within, rather than between, industries. In the next part of this chapter, we shall discuss the conceptual and measurement problems arising from the statistical definition of 'industries'.

We were attracted to this study by two main developments. First, we discovered that the magnitude of intra-industry trade is empirically significant and has increased substantially in recent years. We document this significance in Chapters 3 and 9 and refer to the existing literature in which intra-industry trade has been measured and analysed. In our judgement the phenomenon has not been given the attention by international trade economists that its magnitude warrants. Second, we found in the economics literature of the sixties the development of some theoretical models of international trade and of production, which are suitable for the explanation of intra-industry trade. It turns out that intra-industry trade provides a useful focus for the synthesis and integration of a set of otherwise unrelated international trade models. We hope that this book will succeed

---

[1] Some writers, for example Kojima (1964, 1971), use the terms 'horizontal trade' and 'vertical trade' in place of our terms 'intra-industry' and 'inter-industry' trade. We use the terms 'horizontal' and 'vertical' trade in Chapter 6 in the different sense of trade in competing products and the exchange of products at different stages of production.

in proving the existence of a phenomenon deserving greater attention and, at the same time, make some progress in the analysis of it.

The plan of this book is as follows. In the remaining sections of this chapter, we discuss some conceptual problems arising from the definition of an industry. The last sections of this chapter are devoted to a survey of the theory of intra-industry trade which is designed to show how our ideas fit into the existing literature on international economics.

In Part I we develop a statistical measure for the quantification of the intra-industry trade phenomenon and discuss its theoretical properties. In Chapter 3 intra-industry trade is measured using both time-series and cross-sectional data for ten OECD countries. We also review empirical studies of intra-industry trade in south-east Asia and Yugoslavia. The sensitivity of the measure to aggregation is tested with disaggregated data of Australian trade in Chapter 4. Part II contains theoretical models capable of explaining intra-industry trade. We note that these models predict other characteristics of trade and production; in particular the similarity across countries of commodity export and production. In Part III we analyse the implications of trade in differentiated products for such traditional international trade topics as gains from trade, customs unions and foreign investment. The book closes with some tests of the theoretical models presented in Part II. Because of data limitations most of the tests are indirect. However, we also present the results of some rather inconclusive direct tests we have made and outline some promising hypotheses on which future empirical work might be based.

THE CONCEPT OF AN INDUSTRY

Formulations of the Heckscher–Ohlin model use the term industry as an agglomeration of firms which produce a perfectly homogeneous commodity such as 'cloth' or 'wheat'. This concept of an 'industry' is adequate to explain the existence of international trade but all empirical studies involving this theoretical concept run into the following problem.

Goods and services possess large numbers of characteristics, in the sense of Lancaster (1966), and no two are ever perfect substitutes for each other with respect to all characteristics. Therefore, for analytical and statistical purposes it is necessary to aggregate the production, trade and consumption of goods and services into sets. The criteria of aggregation used in the compilation of international trade statistics are the extent of commodities' substitutability in consumption and the similarity of input requirements in production. At the 2-digit and, in some cases, at the 3-digit level of aggregation of the Standard Industrial Trade Classification (SITC), the resultant aggregates of internationally traded goods correspond roughly to 'industries', as the concept is used conventionally in economic analysis, that is, a group of producers producing essentially the same set of commodities. International trade statistics at these levels of aggregation show a surprisingly high level of simultaneous export and import of goods and services of the same industry, as we show in Part I.

Empirical tests of the Heckscher–Ohlin model, and econometric estimates of trade elasticities, have tended to identify sets of commodities as grouped in the accepted classification of trade statistics with the industry of the Heckscher–Ohlin model, which is assumed to produce only a single perfectly homogeneous commodity. They have, therefore, tended to disregard the problems arising from the obvious discrepancy between the industry, as defined in the model underlying the hypothesis tested, and the industry as defined in the aggregated data. The usual approach has been to consider only *net* exports or imports as the relevant magnitude of trade.[2] This practice has correctly been attributed to the problem of aggregation but no analysis of the appropriate choice of aggregation levels is presented, nor has the sensitivity of the results to aggregation been tested. These investigations do not appear to have faced squarely the fact that a given industry's simultaneous exports and imports is inconsistent with the premise of the theory they set out to test.

There is a second objection to those tests of the models of comparative advantage and calculations of elasticities which net exports and imports. This netting removes a large part of the total value of flows of exports and imports which are being explained. In fact, the measure of intra-industry trade which we

[2] See, for example, MacDougall (1951), Balassa (1963), Leamer and Stern (1970) and Baldwin (1971).

use in this study tells us, as a by-product, the percentage of total trade flows which are removed by netting. This is so because we define intra-industry trade as the exports of an industry which are matched by a corresponding value of imports, or vice versa. The measures reported in Chapter 3 show that 63 per cent of the total trade of ten major OECD countries, recorded at the 3-digit level of the SITC, were matching exports and imports. That is, the netting of exports and imports at this commonly used level of aggregation removes 63 per cent of the value of the total observations.

The results reported in this book suggest the necessity of two developments if we are to explain international trade flows. First, we must disaggregate the trade data so that exports and imports are not included in the same aggregate. This means we should cease netting imports and exports but it does not imply that we should disaggregate until we find no simultaneous exports and imports within trade classification items. For many purposes it will be useful to examine the trade data at a level which shows exports and imports of a set of commodities called an 'industry'. What must be recognised is that in multiproduct industries comparative costs must be specified in terms of individual commodities and not industries. Producers in a multiproduct industry have cost advantages in some commodities relative to producers in other countries and have simultaneously comparative cost disadvantages in other commodities.

The second need in international trade studies is to consider models other than the standard Heckscher–Ohlin model, which allow new determinants of international trade, and in particular trade in differentiated products. This aspect is discussed in the next section.

We decided that it serves the purposes of our study best if we cease the search for an unambiguous definition of an industry at some level of aggregation and instead call each statistical class of internationally traded goods, regardless of the level of aggregation, an 'industry'. Thus we employ the somewhat unusual terminology of referring to industries manufacturing 'Ski boots' and 'Sand shoes', which are part of the industry producing 'Shoes, gaiters and similar articles'. (Chapter 2 gives a description of actual classification schemes in use.) Our unconventional use of the term 'industry' may cause initial difficulty for readers accustomed to considering an industry as a group of firms producing a fixed range of products but this pragmatic definition allows us, without further terminological preliminaries, to examine the pattern of export and import trade of countries at several different levels of aggregation. In fact, however, most of the empirical analysis concentrates on the 3-digit and, if that is not possible, the 2-digit level of the trade statistics, which corresponds most closely to the conventional definition of an industry as a set of producers competing in the production of the same set of commodities. This level of aggregation is appropriate to an examination of the hypotheses suggested by the models of industry behaviour which are outlined in Part II.

INTRA-INDUSTRY TRADE AND TRADITIONAL THEORY

The mainstream of theory in international economics over the past forty years, which has been used to explain international trade patterns, gains from trade, costs of protection, etc., has been based on the assumptions that production of each commodity is subject to constant returns to scale and that markets for commodities and factors are perfectly competitive. These assumptions in turn are founded on important theoretical and empirical evidence. First, few empirical studies of production have been able to discover evidence of the existence of significant and widespread economies of scale obtainable from different sizes of plants. Indirectly this evidence of constant returns to scale seems to be supported by the fact that the production of commodities entering into international trade typically has not led to complete specialisation so that imported products of a given industry supplement, rather than replace, totally domestic production. The existence of constant or diminishing returns explains this phenomenon even if the domestic and foreign products are perfect substitutes.

Second, while perfect competition is only an abstraction, the existence of free markets in capitalist economies results in the operation of market forces guiding the behaviour of producers and consumers and this is the most important characteristic of the model of perfect competition. For this reason the assumption of perfect competition has been considered a most useful abstraction for many of the problems analysed by international trade theory.

Recently, however, Johnson (1968, 1969) suggested that refinements and extensions of the trade models based on these two assumptions, but also taking into account more factors and products, technical change, dynamic growth, etc., have begun to run into seriously diminishing returns and that useful understanding of international trade problems can be expected to be gained more readily by including economies of scale in production and product markets which are imperfectly competitive. Some such extensions have been attempted before and have resulted in a useful and somewhat neglected body of analytical tools and propositions.[3] They have never been important because of the lack of evidence of economies of scale cited above and because the complexity of the analysis resulted in few testable propositions about international trade patterns.

In the last decade there have been three important and independent strands of research which have lowered or removed these barriers to success of the decreasing cost and imperfect competition models of international trade. These are:

1 New evidence of economies of scale.
2 Observations of the effects of trade liberalisation.
3 New applications of imperfect competition.

ECONOMIES OF SCALE

First, and in a sense more fundamentally, understanding of the nature of economies of scale has increased and empirical evidence concerning their existence has been produced. It is possible to distinguish three sources of economies in a given industry: size of plants, length of production runs and size of firms.[4] These sources of economies arise because, in almost every

[3] On economies of scale in the theory of international trade, see Chipman (1965, especially pp. 739–49), Caves (1960, pp. 160–78). On imperfect competition in the theory of international trade, see Johnson (1967, Chapter 7, and 1968, pp. 12–14).

[4] These variables may be regarded as arguments of the cost functions for individual commodities in addition to the input prices. There are of course other variables that may affect unit costs. There may be dynamic economies of scale. It is also often alleged that there are cost advantages to producers in large economies. These advantages are traceable to

industry, there are a number of firms typically operating several plants, each of which commonly produces a range of products.

The classic category of economies of scale resulting in reduction in unit costs are economies which are a function of the scale of input of either an entire industry or of individual plants. This scale has been measured by the number of employees, value-added, output capacity or some other measure of size of plants producing a fixed mix of standardised products. They are considered to arise for two reasons. The first and most generally accepted reason is the existence of indivisibilities of capital equipment or of the skills of workers who operate them. At higher levels of output it is possible to introduce machines which are more efficient because they are special-purpose or more-automated. Second, there are costs which increase less than proportionately with output. For example, the decline in physical inputs per unit of output in the use of containers of pipelines whose capacity is given by volume while costs are a function of the surface area. These relationships occur in industries that utilise liquids or gas inputs – such as the petroleum-refining, fertiliser and chemical industries – as has been shown in studies of engineering production functions (see Smith (1961)). While these economies of scale associated with the size of plant have received most attention in the theoretical literature, many empirical studies have found little or no relationship between plant size and labour productivity. They have also found that within an industry, there coexists plants of widely varying sizes.[5] These findings have usually been interpreted as showing there are no significant economies of plant size.

More recently these results have been interpreted as revealing that the most important determinant of productivity or unit costs is not the size of plant but how production is organised within a plant of a given size.[6] This finding is very important for

economies, of one of the three types discussed here, in some unit of production, or to the availability of specialised services such as advertising, computer and financial services which are sometimes not available in smaller economies.

[5] For a discussion of some empirical findings and their interpretation, see Daly *et al.* (1968) and Balassa (1967).

[6] For example, Daly *et al.* (1968, p. 20), Wonnacott and Wonnacott (1967, pp. 38, 175–82) and Verdoorn (1960, p. 346).

our analysis because, as we shall show, it implies a different pattern of international specialisation than if the economies are functionally related to the size of plant. The distinction is particularly relevant to the multiproduct plant or firm in imperfectly competitive industries, which have been generally ignored by theorists who assumed that each plant or firm produces only one standardised product. In the smaller domestic markets of Canada and of individual West European countries, over a wide range of manufacturing industries, individual plants produce a larger range of products, and have shorter production runs than in the United States.[7]

These longer production runs in the United States result in lower unit costs because they require less frequent halts in production to set or adjust machinery, less 'downtime' to move different models or products through production lines, more specialisation in labour and capital equipment, and smaller inventories of inputs and output. If protection of domestic industries in two countries results in both countries producing the same range of products in an industry, the smaller aggregate output and smaller number of plants in the smaller of the two countries means that all plants have shorter production runs and, as a consequence, higher unit costs of production. This difference in length of production runs apparently explains much of the difference between Canadian and US labour productivities for comparable industries.

Even though one may find economies of scale related to the size of plant and to the length of the production run, it does not follow necessarily that these economies of scale can be captured by increased size of firms. A large firm size may permit longer production runs only if the firm does not produce a correspondingly wider range of goods or models than smaller firms in the industry. There may be further economies or diseconomies related to the size of the company itself. There may be increasing unit costs due to higher costs of administration and control within the firm. Or, there may be reductions in the unit costs of materials or components purchased, or in administration, or warehousing.

It is worth emphasising that under the assumption of perfect

[7] Daly *et al.* (1968) and Lloyd (1971, pp. 61–4) cite some evidence for Canada and New Zealand respectively.

competition and the normal assumptions about an industry producing one homogeneous product, the concept of economies of scale due to length of runs can be fitted in only with great difficulty. Under imperfect competition assumptions, on the other hand, the production of quality- and style-differentiated products in the same plant, and the opportunity to reap economies from specialisation and increased length of runs, follow directly. While dynamic economies of scale occur in the production of both homogeneous and monopolistically differentiated products, their empirical significance is likely to be greater in monopolistic and oligopolistic industries where competition leads to frequent changes in the style or quality of products.

EFFECTS OF TRADE LIBERALISATION

A second strand of recent research has shown that the neglect of market structure can lead to inadequate predictions about the growth of international trade and welfare, following economic integration. During the fifties several studies attempted to predict the increase in trade resulting from general tariff reductions and especially the mutual tariff concessions contemplated by the countries of the proposed European Economic Community.[8] These studies were based on econometric estimates of price elasticities of demand for the products of specific industries; such estimates in turn were based on price and quantity observations drawn from periods during which factors other than tariff changes mainly influenced price variations. These estimates predicted increases in international trade which in part turned out to be much too low.

A closer examination of the actual increase in trade among the members of the Benelux by Verdoorn (1960), and of the EEC by Balassa (1963, 1966), Grubel (1967) and Adler (1970), showed that much of it had taken place not through greater national specialisation in the production and export of individual 'industries', as the estimates of gains had assumed, but through increased trade in products belonging to the same industry. Because of the similarity of material input requirements of the products from the same industry and the quite similar resource endowments of the countries of the EEC it is analytically

[8] See Johnson (1958), Krause (1963a and b) and Janssen (1961).

difficult to explain the marked increase in this intra-industry trade by use of the traditional Heckscher–Ohlin model of comparative advantage. This is true even if one, more accurately, states comparative advantage in terms of individual commodities rather than industries. While the growth in intra-industry trade itself is not proof of the existence of imperfect competition and economies of scale, the analysis of Part II will show that assumptions about the existence of economies of scale of the type discussed above, and about the dynamic interpenetration of markets by oligopolists after mutual tariff reductions, result in the prediction of events closely resembling those actually observed in the formation of the EEC.

IMPERFECT COMPETITION MODELS

A third, important set of recent academic research projects has resulted in the formulation of useful empirical propositions about the pattern of international trade in monopolistically differentiated products. The parts of these studies relevant to the present analysis of intra-industry trade will be presented with analytical rigour in the next chapters. At this point their main contributions are summarised briefly.

First, Linder (1961, pp. 87–91) hypothesised and found that a country like Sweden tends to specialise in the production and export of such *quality* products as are demanded by the country's income class with the largest numbers. Product qualities demanded by income groups with smaller numbers typically are imported from countries where the appropriate income is enjoyed by the largest proportion of the population. Drèze (1960, 1961) developed a related model, except that he emphasised the *style* and *design* differences in products. He found that small countries with a population of ethnic and cultural diversity, such as Belgium, are unable to produce styles and designs of goods to meet the demands of their population at prices competitive with imports from abroad. Instead, Belgium imports style-specific products from its larger, neighbouring countries and specialises in the production of more standardised and functional variants in demand by a narrow section of the market in the rest of the world.

Studies by Posner (1961), Hufbauer (1966) and Vernon

(1966)[9] have resulted in the specification of models capable of explaining international trade in new products in which the producing country has a comparative advantage due to patent or copyright protection or the existence of dynamic economies of scale. Since, at the present level of industrialisation in the world, most 'new' products have close competitive substitutes, these models of 'technological gaps' and 'product-cycle' trade are directly applicable to the theory of intra-industry trade.

IMPERFECT COMPETITION AND INTERNATIONAL
  CAPITAL FLOWS

It is useful to note at this point that the extensions of international trade theory through changes in the assumptions about economies of scale and the nature of competition have their parallel in the recent developments in the theory of international capital flows. The existing theory of international capital flows implies that financial capital moves to countries where the marginal productivity of real assets is the highest. This theory leaves unexplained two empirically important real world phenomena.

First, the largest proportion of all international capital flows are in the form of direct investment, and second, direct investment and some forms of financial capital are simultaneously imported and exported by many countries. The first phenomenon is left unexplained by the existing theory because, if a profitable investment opportunity exists in a given country, a local entrepreneur should be able to exploit it by borrowing abroad unless there is an additional theoretical argument suggesting that he suffers from a comparative disadvantage relative to the foreign entrepreneur. The second phenomenon is analogous to the intra-industry trade. In the existing theory a country cannot simultaneously have a relatively high and low rate of return to capital in comparison with the rest of the world. Both deficiencies arise because capital is treated as a homogeneous rather than a heterogeneous flow.

The explanations of these real world phenomenon were accomplished successfully through the extensions of the pure capital-flow model into a world where economies of scale,

[9] See also Hirsch (1967).

imperfect competition and uncertainty play an essential role. For an excellent review and synthesis of the literature in this field the reader is referred to Caves (1971). In Chapter 9 we shall discuss in greater detail the relationship between the theory of intra-industry trade and international capital flows.

HISTORICAL ANTECEDENTS TO THE STUDY OF INTRA-INDUSTRY TRADE

The study of intra-industry trade presented in this book can be looked upon as the continuation of a past concern with the pattern of commodity trade. The idea of intra-industry trade is not new. The growing exchange of manufactures for manufactures has been recognised for some time. What is new is the realisation of the extent of this trade, its causes and an awareness of its policy implications. Earlier studies can be separated into three groups, each of which has been stimulated by a different analytical problem or question of policy.

The first group of studies was concerned with the geographic distribution of trade. It arose out of the international trade practices developed during the depression of the thirties. At that time countries engaged widely in bilateral trade agreements in order to overcome the adverse effects of exchange-rate uncertainty and beggar-thy-neighbour policies and to increase the effectiveness of domestic employment policies. These trade agreements resulted in lower levels of world trade and efficiency, the extent of which is related to the magnitude of bilateral and multilateral balancing of trade flows. The League of Nations published a series of studies quantifying the value of trade balanced in these ways (1933, 1934, 1935, 1936, 1942).

The author of many of these studies was Hilgerdt, who extended and refined the analysis in other studies (1935, 1943). One of the main analytical tools of his analysis was the separation of a country's total merchandise trade into flows which were balanced by bilateral imports and exports and by multilateral surpluses and deficits.[10] These bilateral and multilateral balances are analytically analogous to the balance of exports

[10] The precise nature of the statistical measures is discussed in Chapter 2 below. The study of bilateral and multilateral trade balancing was recently updated by Michaely (1962b).

and imports in the same commodity class, which is called intra-industry trade, and to the surpluses and deficits in each class, which are called inter-industry trade.

The second group of studies was concerned with the historic development of the commodity distribution of trade, especially with respect to the trade of foodstuffs and raw materials for manufactures. This concern was based on the widely held belief that economic development in 'agricultural' countries would reduce their demand for manufactures from the already industrialised countries, which would then find it difficult to pay for their imports of foodstuffs and raw materials. The two most important studies of this problem were by Hilgerdt (1945) and Hirschman (1945).[11]

The analytical approach of these studies was to compute measures reflecting the extent to which trade involved the exchange of first, manufactures for manufactures; second, manufactures for foodstuffs and raw materials; and third, foodstuffs and raw materials for foodstuffs and raw materials. After about thirty years of rapid economic development and the failure of the feared problem to arise, it comes as no surprise to present-day economists that the studies by Hilgerdt and Hirschman should have found that in the pre-World War II period there was already substantial trade in manufactures for manufactures, which Hirschman considered to be evidence of 'the division of labour between national industries' (Hirschman, 1945, p. 126). Again the analytical approach of these studies involving the matching of individual countries' exports and imports by classes of commodities is equivalent to the problem of intra-industry trade with only two industries – 'manufactures' and 'foodstuffs and raw materials'.

In another study Frankel noted: 'We frequently meet the phenomenon that countries with a relatively high proportion of international trade per head of population export and import what are apparently the same commodities' (Frankel, 1943, p. 195). He explained such trade in terms of differences in quality between the imported and exported goods. While he did not attempt to measure the extent of this trade he did attempt to measure quality differences by comparing the unit values of comparable export and import goods and cited many examples

[11] This was reproduced as Chapter 7 of Hirschman (1945).

of countries specialising in the production of a certain quality
of a good. Further, he attributed this specialisation to differences in the human skills in the labourers of different countries:
'We may make a general statement that the more a country is
industrialised the better it can produce goods of higher quality'
(p. 195).

A variant of the concern over the historic development of
trade in manufactures for foodstuffs and raw materials has
occupied, among others, Baldwin (1958[12]), Maizels (1963) and
Kojima (1962, 1964, 1971), who were concerned principally to
explain inter-country differences in the rates of growth in the
export of manufactures. This problem has important implications for countries encountering balance of payments deficits
and for development strategies generally. These writers pointed
out that the exchange of manufactures for manufactures among
the industrial developed countries of West Europe and North
America was increasing in importance and accounted for most
of the expansion of trade among these countries. Of these
studies, the reasoning and method of those by Kojima are closest
to those discussed in this book. Kojima defined eight categories
of internationally traded goods according to differences in their
resource-, capital- and labour-intensity. He found that simultaneous imports and exports of goods within the same class were
relatively high in all the large industrial countries and that, during
the late fifties, trade within the category of capital-intensive
heavy and chemical goods had expanded considerably more
rapidly than total world trade. The similarity of his approach
to the approach used in intra-industry trade analysis is obvious.

Kojima used these empirical findings as a basis for some
suggestions of a theory of dynamic comparative advantage
based on the importance of economies of scale, technical change
and product differentiation. He also suggested that the growth
of trade in similar products indicated the desirability of closer
economic cooperation (Kojima, 1966, and Kojima (ed.), 1968,
especially pp. 160–63).[13] These topics are discussed at length in
the following chapters.

---

[12] Baldwin gives a number of references to related studies.

[13] Drysdale (Kojima (ed.), 1968, pp. 194–223 and 1969) has made a
similar argument for Australian participation in a Pacific Free Trade
Area. These views are discussed in Chapter 9.

The third group of studies was stimulated by international trade problems accompanying economic integration after World War II. As noted already, Verdoorn (1960), Balassa (1963, 1966), Adler (1970) and Grubel (1967) analysed the effects of mutual tariff reductions on the patterns of specialisation. It was in this context that the concepts of intra- and inter-industry trade proper were developed and the theoretical implications of the rapid growth in intra-industry trade for several well-known propositions from international trade theory were raised. This book represents an effort to provide a more rigorous analysis of the phenomenon of intra-industry trade and to measure it in a context other than economic integration.

Part I Measurement of the Intra-Industry Trade Phenomenon

2 Measures of Intra-Industry Trade

The present chapter consists of three parts. The first contains a schematic representation of data available for the measurement of intra-industry trade. The second part presents the summary measure of intra-industry trade which we use and some discussion of its statistical properties. In the third part alternative measures of intra-industry trade are analysed.

AVAILABLE INTERNATIONAL TRADE DATA

Under the Standard International Trade Classification (SITC), countries have adopted identical descriptions and coverages for the recording of international trade at the 1-, 2-, 3- and 5-digit levels of aggregation. However, at the lowest levels of aggregation of 7 digits, individual countries are free to choose their own descriptions and coverages. In Fig. 2.1, we present in schematic form an example of the classification of a small set of commodities at each level of aggregation. The 7-digit items are from the Australian export and imports classifications. Other countries' statistics at the 7-digit level are similar to those of Australia.

Each statistical class of traded goods, regardless of the level of aggregation for the purposes of this study, is considered to represent the trade of an 'industry', as mentioned in Chapter 1. This implies that there exists, for example, a ski-boot industry, which is part of an industry producing footwear with leather uppers, etc., as can be seen from Fig. 2.1. The coverage of exports and imports under the SITC is identical.

For the purposes of measuring intra-industry specialisation exports and imports should both be measured f.o.b., or both c.i.f. Of the two, f.o.b. valuations are preferable because they measure the value of trade produced by producers in each industry, excluding the value added by international transporters of the home countries or of some third foreign country. In the statistical measure we shall employ, c.i.f. values give the

Figure 2.1
Schematic Presentation of Trade Classification

Digits	Industries		
7	851.02.03 Ski boots	851.02.07 Sand shoes, rubber-soled	851.02.08 Sand shoes, other soles
5	851.02 Footwear with leather uppers, soles of rubber or plastic		851.03 Footwear with soles of wood or cork
3	851 Shoes	852 Gaiters	
2	85 Footwear, gaiters and similar articles	82 Furniture	84 Clothing and clothing accessories
1	8 Miscellaneous manufactured articles		

same magnitude as f.o.b. values only if the margins for costs of insurance and freight are the same for export and import goods. For countries that value exports f.o.b. and imports c.i.f. the measures may be biased upwards or downwards, depending mainly on whether exports of commodities are greater or less than imports in the aggregate.

THE PROPOSED MEASURE OF INTRA-INDUSTRY TRADE

Intra-industry trade (R_i) is defined as the value of exports of an 'industry' which is exactly matched by the imports of the same industry, that is,

$$R_i = (X_i + M_i) - |X_i - M_i| \qquad (2.1)$$

where X_i and M_i are the value of the exports and imports of industry valued in the home country's currency[1] and $i = 1, \ldots n$, where n is the number of industries at a chosen level of aggregation. R_i can be calculated for the home country's trade with one, or a subset, or all foreign countries. Inter-industry trade is defined as

$$S_i = |X_i - M_i| \qquad (2.2)$$

It is clear that intra-industry trade is the value of total trade $(X_i + M_i)$ remaining after subtraction of net exports or imports of the industry $|X_i - M_i|$.

[1] Alternatively, R_i may be taken as the lesser of the values of exports and imports multiplied by two.

To facilitate comparisons of these measures for different industries and countries it is useful to express them as a percentage of each industry's combined exports and imports. The resultant measures of inter- and intra-industry trade are respectively

$$A_i = [|X_i - M_i|/(X_i + M_i)] \cdot 100 \qquad (2.3)$$

and

$$B_i = [(X_i + M_i) - |X_i - M_i|] \, 100/(X_i + M_i) \qquad (2.4)$$

Both measures vary between 0 and 100. Since the level of inter-industry trade is always given by 100 minus the measured level of intra-industry trade all further discussion is in terms of intra-industry trade, B_i. Because the measure B_i is used intensively in the following chapters it may be useful to show what values it takes in some examples.

When the exports are exactly equal to imports of an industry, B_i is 100. When there are exports but no imports, or vice versa, the measure is 0, which is desirable. When exports are equal to one-half of imports, or vice versa, the measure is 66·6 per cent. That is, the value matching exports and imports is $\frac{2}{3}$ of the total value of exports plus imports.

When the measures of intra-industry trade are calculated for all individual industries at all levels of aggregation the analysis of these measures proceeds in two directions. First, at a given level of aggregation we examine the distribution of these measures among some or all individual industries; and second, for a particular set of traded goods we examine the measures of intra-industry trade computed at different levels of aggregation.

Concerning the first direction of analysis, the most useful statistic for summarising the distribution of a set of individual measures is the mean, using as weights the relative size of exports plus imports of each industry in the total value of exports plus imports of the set of n industries:

$$\bar{B}_i = \sum_i^n B_i(X_i + M_i)/\sum_i^n (X_i + M_i) \cdot 100$$

$$= \frac{\sum_i^n (X_i + M_i) - \sum_i^n |X_i - M_i|}{\sum_i^n (X_i + M_i)} \cdot 100 \qquad (2.5)$$

$\bar{B}_i$ measures average intra-industry trade directly as a percentage of the export plus import trade. It is also equal to the sum of the intra-industry trade for the industries as a percentage of the total export plus import trade of the n industries:

$$\bar{B}_i = \frac{\sum_i^n [(X_i + M_i) - |X_i - M_i|]}{\sum_i^n (X_i + M_i)} \cdot 100 \qquad (2.6)$$

THE MEASURE AND BIAS FROM TRADE IMBALANCE

The mean is a biased downward measure of intra-industry trade if the country's total commodity trade is imbalanced or if the mean is an average of some subset of all industries for which exports are not equal to imports. With an imbalance between exports and imports the mean must be less than 100 no matter what the pattern of exports and imports, because exports cannot match imports in every industry. This is an undesirable feature of a measure of average intra-industry trade which is due to the fact that it captures both the trade imbalance and the strength of the intra-industry trade.

When considering all commodity trade we must adjust for the aggregate trade imbalance by expressing intra-industry trade as a proportion of total commodity export plus import trade less the trade imbalance. This gives the adjusted measure

$$\bar{C}_i = \frac{\sum_i^n (X_i + M_i) - \sum_i^n |X_i - M_i|}{\sum_i^n (X_i + M_i) - |\sum_i^n X_i - \sum_i^n M_i|} \cdot 100 \qquad (2.7)$$

where n is the total number of industries at the chosen level of aggregation. Clearly

$$\bar{C}_i = \bar{B}_i \cdot \frac{\sum_i^n (X_i + M_i)}{\sum_i^n (X_i + M_i) - |\sum_i^n X_i - \sum_i^n M_i|}$$

$$= \bar{B}_i \cdot 1/(1 - k) \qquad (2.8)$$

where

$$k = \frac{|\sum_i^n X_i - \sum_i^n M_i|}{\sum_i^n (X_i + M_i)}$$

Thus the adjustment factor and the adjusted measure increase as the trade imbalance increases as a proportion of total export plus import trade.

When the measures relate to trade with individual countries this adjustment makes a substantial difference if the bilateral trade imbalances are large relative to the combined total export and import trade. For example, if the trade deficit (surplus) is equal to one-tenth or one-fifth of the value of export plus import trade the adjustment increases the measure by one-ninth or one-quarter respectively. For trade with a given country or with all countries this adjustment increases the average measures by the same proportion at all levels of aggregation. The adjusted measures lie in the closed interval [0, 100].

THE MEASURE AND AGGREGATION

The second direction of analysis involves the comparison of the B_is at different levels of aggregation. For the ith industry, *at a particular level of aggregation*, X_i and M_i are each made up of the exports and imports of industries defined at a more disaggregated level (that is, a higher level of the SITC), called X_{ij} and M_{ij} respectively. The percentage of intra-industry trade for the ith industry is calculated by using the sums $\Sigma_j X_{ij}$ and $\Sigma_j M_{ij}$. From equation (2.4)

$$B_i = \frac{\Sigma_j(X_{ij}+M_{ij}) - |\Sigma_j X_{ij} - \Sigma_j M_{ij}|}{\Sigma_j(X_{ij}+M_{ij})} \cdot 100 \qquad (2.9)$$

It is important to note the following result of this aggregation. Since[2]

$$R_i = \Sigma_j(X_{ij}+M_{ij}) - |\Sigma_j X_{ij} - \Sigma_j M_{ij}| \\ \geqslant \Sigma_j(X_{ij}+M_{ij}) - \Sigma_j|X_{ij} - M_{ij}| \qquad (2.10)$$

and since the denominator of B_i is unaffected by aggregation the measure of intra-industry trade at a more aggregative level is greater than, or at least no less than, the measured intra-industry trade with a finer commodity breakdown. Aggregation increases the measure of intra-industry trade by an amount in proportion to the extent to which the terms $(X_{ij} - M_{ij})$ at the less aggregated level are of opposite sign. Indeed in the extreme

[2] The inequality follows from the generalised triangle inequality $\Sigma_i a_i$ | $\leqslant \Sigma |a_i|$, where a_i are real numbers.

case it is possible that an aggregated measure is 100 when at the disaggregated level the *j* measures are zero.

This effect of aggregation also applies to aggregation across countries, at a given SITC digit level. Therefore the weighted average of the measures of bilateral trade with individual countries, with each country's weights determined by its share of the total export plus import trade, is less than the measure for intra-industry trade between the country and all other countries combined. Another implication of the special aggregation property of our measure is that, at any level of aggregation, it provides a *maximum* estimate of the measure for the same trade flows of a lower level of aggregation.

The empirical study of Australian data in Chapter 4 produces some knowledge about the sensitivity of the intra-industry trade measure to aggregation of the trade data.

ALTERNATIVE MEASURES OF TRADE PATTERNS

The measures of inter- and intra-industry trade presented in the preceding section were developed after consideration of several alternative measures which have arisen in the analysis of different but analogous problems. Any of the measures could be applied to any problem of measuring the extent of 'similarity' or 'matching' between two sets of figures, trade flows or other values.

Verdoorn (1960) measured the strength of inter- and intra-industry specialisation by computing, for all industries at the 3-digit level, the ratio U_i:

$$U_i = \frac{X_i}{M_i} \tag{2.11}$$

X_i and M_i in his study were Dutch exports to, and imports from, Belgium–Luxembourg. This ratio varies between 0 and $+\infty$. If the ratio for a given industry considered over time moved towards unity, intra-industry specialisation was considered to take place. If the ratio over time diverged from unity, inter-industry specialisation took place.

The obvious disadvantage of this measure is that any fraction $1/m$ and its inverse m should measure the same degree of inequality of intra-industry specialisation. However, the frequency distribution of the ratios and the statistics of these distributions such as the mean will differ according as the ratio is defined as X_i/M_i or M_i/X_i. This is an undesirable property which arises because all observations less than unity are concentrated between zero and unity.

Kojima (1964) and Grubel (1967) also measured the degree of inter- and intra-industry specialisation by calculating ratios of exports and imports. Grubel made all numbers greater than one by taking the ratio of the larger of the export and import values to the smaller. Under this measure intra-industry specialisation grew through time if the ratios moved towards unity, and decreased if they diverged from unity. Kojima used the reciprocal ratio of the smaller value to the larger value. The values of this statistic lie between 0 and 1, and his measure moves towards unity as intra-industry grows.

While this method of quantifying the relationship between imports and exports of the one industry overcame one undesirable feature of the Verdoorn measure it had a major shortcoming. It did not provide a direct measure of the proportion of the intra-industry trade for all industries, as does the measure adapted for the present study.[3]

Hirschman (1945) examined world exports and imports of the two categories of goods, manufactures and raw materials–foodstuffs. He divided the international trade of a country into three components:

1 The aggregate trade balance, i.e. the excess of imports over exports, or exports over imports, in commodity trade.
2 The value of matching exports and imports of manufactures and of raw materials–foodstuffs.
3 The value of exports or imports of raw materials and foodstuffs which is matched by imports or exports of manufactures, and vice versa.

He then expressed these components as percentages of total export plus import trade. The second measure is the same as the

[3] There are one-to-one correspondences between both measures previously used by Kojima and Grubel and our measure, B_i. If the lesser of the values of exports and imports is expressed as a percentage of the greater, V_i, then the function relating V_i and B_i is $B_i = 2V_i/1 + V_i$. This function transforms the relative values of intra-industry trade and provides a direct measure of the percentage of intra-industry trade.

unadjusted measure of intra-industry trade $\bar{B}_i$ presented above for the case of two industries.[4]

Balassa (1966) defined his measure of intra-industry trade as

$$\bar{D}_i = (1/n) \sum_i^n \left[\frac{|X_i - M_i|}{X_i + M_i} \right] \qquad (2.12)$$

This is the unweighted average of the ratios $|X_i - M_i|/(X_i + M_i)$. These industry ratios, and their average $\bar{D}_i$, really measure inter-industry trade as previously defined. Balassa interpreted it as a measure of intra-industry trade, the importance of intra-industry increasing as the measure decreases. $\bar{D}_i$ also lies between limits 0 and 1. Balassa's measure has two drawbacks. First, it gives equal weight to all industries, irrespective of whether their share in total industry exports plus imports is large or small. Second, there is no correction for the aggregate trade imbalance.

Michaely (1962a) used an index of dissimilarity in the commodity composition of a country's export and import trade in order to study the relationship between the composition of exports and imports on the one hand and fluctuations in the commodity terms of trade on the other. In symbols defined above, his measure is

$$\bar{E}_i = \sum_i^n \left| \frac{X_i}{\sum_i^n X_i} - \frac{M_i}{\sum_i^n M_i} \right| \qquad (2.13)$$

This index varies between limits of 0 (complete similarity) and 2 (complete dissimilarity). If the aggregate value of exports is equal to the aggregate value of imports his measure is exactly double the value of our measure. If aggregate exports are not equal to aggregate imports, Michaely's procedure provides an alternative way of removing the influence of the trade im-

---

[4] Hufbauer (1974) uses the measure, in our symbols, $\sum_i |X_i - M_i|/\sum_i Q_i$, where Q_i is value added in the ith product, to measure 'specialisation', i.e. inter-industry specialisation. This may be regarded as the product of two measures, $\sum_i |X_i - M_i|/\sum_i (X_i + M_i)$ and $\sum_i (X_i + M_i)/\sum_i Q_i$. Hence it combines a measure of the pattern of trade with a measure of the value of trade in relation to value-added.

balance.[5] The measure is easier to interpret it if is multiplied by $\frac{1}{2}$ so that it varies between 0 and 1. The corresponding measure of intra-commodity trade is then obtained by subtracting the Michaely measure of inter-commodity trade (adjusted by the factor $\frac{1}{2}$) from unity:

$$F_i = 1 - \tfrac{1}{2} \sum_i^n \left| \frac{X_i}{\sum\limits_i^n X_i} - \frac{M_i}{\sum\limits_i^n M_i} \right| \qquad (2.14)$$

This measure is very close to the adjusted measure $\bar{C}_i$. Indeed if either (1) aggregate exports equal aggregate imports, or (2) exports of each commodity (or industry) are greater (or less) than imports of the same commodity, then the two measures are identical.

The latter case illustrates a slight problem.[6] We see from equations (2.5) and (2.10) that $\bar{C}_i$ is unity if exports exceed imports, or vice versa, for all industries. This is true no matter what the distribution of exports and imports, subject to this constraint. Thus, it holds if, say, the exports of all industries are twice the value of imports or if the exports of some industries are say three times the value of corresponding imports while the exports of others are only 1·1 times the value of imports. If a country has a large imbalance of trade such that exports for most industries exceeded imports, or vice versa, it would be better to use the unadjusted measure $\bar{B}_i$ in preference to $\bar{C}_i$ or $\bar{F}_i$. When reporting the global averages for countries we give in all cases both the adjusted and unadjusted averages.

There is in general a subtle difference between the Michaely measure and $\bar{C}_i$. The Michaely measure is a measure of the extent to which exports as a proportion of total exports offset imports as a proportion of total imports, whereas the measure $\bar{C}_i$ shows the extent of the *absolute* amount of commodity exports offset by imports of the same industries in total commodity trade.[7] For the purpose of examining intra-industry

[5] This is almost certainly Michaely's reason for dividing exports and imports of commodity i by aggregate exports and imports respectively, though he does not give a reason.

[6] Barry Hesketh first pointed out this problem to us.

[7] Michaely (1962b) used the same measure in his study of the country composition trade and multilateral balancing. In this context the concern

trade in the sense of the phenomenon that countries both export and import the same commodities, the measure $\bar{C}_i$ is preferable to $\bar{F}_i$ because $\bar{C}_i$ measures directly the relative importance of matching intra-industry trade.

Further measures have been used in the context of measuring the similarity between the commodity composition of one country's exports and another country's imports or between the commodity composition of exports of pairs of countries. In considering the similarity of one country's exports with that of another country's imports as a possible variable explaining the extent of bilateral trade, Linneman (1966, pp. 140–43) rejected the most obvious of all measures – the correlation coefficient – because it varied from -1 to $+1$. He chose instead the closely related cosine measure.[8] This measures the cosine of the angle between the vectors of exports of commodities and imports of commodities in multicommodity space. Since there is the same number of observations for exports as for imports, it does not matter here whether the exports and imports are the absolute trade figures or normalised as percentages of total exports and imports. This measure could be applied to measure the similarity of a country's export and import trade. In our symbols it would be

$$G_i = \frac{\sum\limits_{i}^{n} (X_i M_i)}{(\sum\limits_{i}^{n} X_i^2 \sum\limits_{i}^{n} M_i^2)^{\frac{1}{2}}} \qquad (2.15)$$

Like several other measures considered, the cosine measure has the desirable property that it varies within the closed interval of 0 to $+1$. However, it generally has a smaller variance among countries than does the measure $\bar{B}_i$, and, unlike these measures, does not record the percentage of intra-industry trade.

---

is with the financing of absolute bilateral imbalances and our measure, perhaps expressed as a percentage of all three components, would seem preferable to his measure which may yield zero measured multilateral balancing when there are substantial bilateral balances. This feature of his index may explain some of his surprising results.

[8] Hufbauer (1971) also used this measure for the same purpose.

3 The Level of Intra-Industry Trade

The statistical measures of intra-industry trade (B_i, $\bar{B}_i$ and $\bar{C}_i$) developed in Chapter 2 are employed in the present chapter to estimate the actual levels of this trade. The chapter falls into different sections which discuss the data and measures for different countries and periods.[1] Statistics published by the Organisation for Economic Cooperation and Development (OECD) are examined to discern patterns of intra-industry trade across countries and industries for the year 1967, and the trends over the period 1959–67. The intra-industry trade of some developing countries is also measured. The sensitivity of the measures of intra-industry trade to changes in the level of aggregation is analysed in Chapter 4.

TOTAL INTRA-INDUSTRY TRADE IN OECD COUNTRIES

Annual statistics of the international trade of its members, at the 3-digit level of the SITC, are published regularly and in convenient tables by the OECD. No other publication systematically presents comparable trade statistics at this level of disaggregation for a number of countries. We employed these data for the countries shown on the horizontal axis of Table 3.1: the EEC countries (Belgium–Luxembourg, Netherlands, West Germany, France and Italy), Canada, US, Japan and Australia. Our primary criterion for selecting these particular countries for study was their dominance of world trade, especially of trade in manufactures. Although this sample is restricted to so-called developed countries, it does contain countries that are quite variable in terms of their participation in regional trading arrangements, the proportion of manufactures in total trade,

[1] In this chapter, we consider only the global trade of individual countries with all other countries. In Chapter 9 there are some estimates of intra-industry trade shares of bilateral trade and trade within regional groups.

their principal trading partners, and other trade characteristics. We included Australia because of its unique characteristics of development and location, the latter providing important natural protection through transport costs.

The year 1967 was the latest for which complete statistics were available at the time we made the calculations. This year ended nearly twenty years of extremely rapid growth in world trade, and progressive lowering of barriers to international trade. The relationship of intra-industry trade and the growth of total trade is discussed below and in Chapter 9.

The two extreme left columns of Table 3.1 give the classification and descriptions of the 3-digit classes. For example, in the important group of industries collected under the 1-digit Section 6, 'Manufactured goods classified chiefly by material', 611 is Leather; 612, Articles of paper, pulp and paperboard; 641, Paper and paperboard; etc. After careful examination we believe that the 3-digit level of the SITC classification corresponds most closely to the usual notion of an industry as a group of producers who produce in the main a common set of commodities.

Before discussing differences in the measured intra-industry trade among countries and among industries it is useful to examine the overall level of intra-industry trade. The last two rows give the percentage of intra-industry trade in the total trade of each of the ten countries, both adjusted and unadjusted for the aggregate trade imbalances of the respective countries. While Verdoorn (1960), Balassa (1966) and Grubel (1967) have drawn attention to the increase in trade within industries since the formation of the EEC, the average intra-industry trade as a percentage of total commodity trade has not previously been measured. The extreme right figure of the last row is the unweighted mean of the intra-industry trade shares of the sample countries. By coincidence the unweighted mean of the intra-industry trade in all industries for these ten countries is 50 per cent.

We can compute exactly the share of the total trade of all ten countries, which is intra-industry trade. This is done simply by adding the total intra-industry trade of each country and dividing by the total trade of these countries. This measure is in symbols as shown on page 36.

TABLE 3.1

Average Intra-Industry Trade, 1967

SITC Classes	Canada	US	Japan	Belgium-Luxembourg	Netherlands	Germany	France	Italy	UK	Australia	Mean†
001 Live animals	64	73	15	94	58	98	89	01	67	58	62
011 Meat, fresh, chilled or frozen	91	48	10	81	28	16	61	01	08	00	34
012 Meat, dried, salted or smoked	85	46	00	52	54	29	66	23	07	00	36
013 Meat in airtight containers, n.e.s., and meat preparations	55	08	86	53	16	22	78	93	71	05	43
022 Milk and cream	20	08	20	68	37	89	04	02	71	00	32
023 Butter	00	32	04	89	06	97	18	03	01	00	25
024 Cheese and curd	90	12	00	41	13	43	61	68	03	37	37
025 Eggs	37	26	14	08	22	03	60	08	66	00	24
031 Fish, fresh and simply preserved	21	15	80	65	43	58	39	08	45	70	44
032 Fish, in airtight containers, n.e.s., and fish preparations	47	51	08	04	95	52	19	01	09	28	31
041 Wheat – including spelt – and meslin, unmilled	*	00	00	20	57	09	50	07	00	05	16
042 Rice	*	00	00	25	54	32	46	04	41	05	19
043 Barley, unmilled	*	35	00	24	86	02	01	00	00	00	21
044 Maize – corn – unmilled	04	01	00	19	09	04	44	02	07	00	08
045 Cereals, unmilled – excl. wheat, rice, barley and maize	18	04	00	10	62	12	34	13	21	00	16
046 Meal and flour of wheat or of meslin	*	*	00	08	96	22	03	01	21	00	19
047 Meal and flour of cereals, except wheat/meslin	37	*	00	26	78	03	25	67	22	00	30
048 Cereal preparations and preparations of flour, fruits and vegetables	68	57	62	64	54	65	63	88	44	21	59
051 Fruit, fresh, and nuts – excl. oil nuts	26	78	18	39	40	02	43	28	01	38	31
052 Dried fruit incl. artificially dehydrated	04	16	00	18	06	05	09	55	00	05	12
053 Fruit, preserved and fruit preparations	33	80	82	44	86	18	68	18	12	09	45
054 Vegetables, roots and tubers, fresh or dried	57	85	12	94	30	13	42	62	14	98	51
055 Vegetables, roots and tubers, preserved or prepared, n.e.s.	67	45	82	93	73	10	78	21	14	41	52
061 Sugar and honey	32	04	02	60	75	26	89	44	20	02	35
062 Sugar confectionery, sugar preparations excl. chocolate confectionery	37	91	42	91	45	55	81	96	18	90	65
071 Coffee	03	04	00	08	34	09	06	01	16	06	9
072 Cocoa	*	01	12	02	96	14	06	40	15	00	21
073 Chocolate and other food preparations containing cocoa, n.e.s.	72	38	43	80	38	44	64	28	99	50	49
074 Tea and mate	26	03	30	74	83	13	00	00	00	01	23
075 Spices	20	16	47	39	84	21	23	20	25	00	30
081 Feeding-stuff for animals – excl. unmilled cereals	61	46	30	44	52	36	59	29	22	89	47
091 Margarine and shortening	21	00	39	93	23	90	06	82	24	00	38
099 Food preparations, n.e.s.	70	78	93	96	36	88	44	100	87	79	77
0 Food and live animals	25	22	15	95	41	22	44	18	14	08	30

Table 3.1 (continued)

SITC Classes	Canada	US	Japan	Belgium–Luxembourg	Nether-lands	Germany	France	Italy	UK	Australia	Mean †
111 Non-alcoholic beverages, n.e.s.	11	31	00	58	41	75	23	05	08	00	25
112 Alcoholic beverages	49	04	65	48	88	58	57	47	64	66	55
121 Tobacco, unmanufactured	25	49	23	07	24	05	06	68	00	01	21
122 Tobacco manufactures	70	11	06	64	76	29	65	08	24	38	39
1 Beverages and tobacco	44	27	28	41	61	28	52	44	43	34	40
211 Hides and skins – excl. fur skins – undressed	68	64	00	87	98	61	58	15	61	04	52
212 Fur skins, undressed	72	59	18	19	32	18	81	02	04	86	39
221 Oil-seeds, oil nuts and oil kernels	75	13	00	17	13	02	18	00	02	34	17
231 Crude rubber – incl. synthetic and reclaimed	88	96	29	18	58	52	62	31	40	04	48
241 Fuel wood and charcoal	66	81	00	19	72	49	19	01	15	00	32
242 Wood in the rough or roughly squared	61	25	00	50	22	32	50	01	06	33	28
243 Wood, shaped or simply worked	14	51	35	19	04	26	31	02	01	18	22
244 Cork, raw and waste	*	04	01	00	00	04	26	52	00	00	10
251 Pulp and waste paper	03	77	28	50	23	15	31	00	03	02	20
261 Silk	15	04	07	00	00	37	18	48	00	00	15
262 Wool and other animal hair	02	12	01	73	59	23	81	04	57	02	33
263 Cotton	14	14	02	19	45	21	03	02	05	03	12
264 Jute	03	00	00	28	63	05	00	01	05	00	12
265 Vegetable fibres, except cotton and jute	41	12	01	87	93	07	91	15	05	00	31
266 Synthetic and regenerated artificial fibres	33	93	23	67	60	39	81	65	65	06	52
267 Waste materials from textile fabrics – incl. rags	*	31	00	57	51	46	69	09	57	15	39
271 Fertilisers, crude	96	20	24	12	07	11	06	00	00	00	7
273 Stone, sand and gravel	13	96	26	92	45	88	93	77	53	91	76
274 Sulphur and unroasted iron pyrites	34	64	05	11	01	20	50	13	02	20	20
275 Natural abrasives – incl. industrial diamonds	23	58	26	98	97	56	42	81	55	08	56
276 Other crude minerals	15	80	05	57	84	61	63	40	98	24	54
281 Iron ore and concentrates	99	27	00	04	05	02	92	07	00	01	15
282 Iron and steel scrap	35	08	00	40	52	74	34	00	00	05	31
283 Ores and concentrates of non-ferrous base metals	62	32	00	11	68	11	07	25	04	71	18
284 Non-ferrous metal scrap	*	73	00	56	11	58	49	09	45	00	49
285 Silver and platinum ores	*	64	00	18	00	01	19	00	01	67	20
286 Ores and concentrates of uranium and thorium	*	00	00	00	00	00	00	00	00	00	00
291 Crude animal materials, n.e.s.	66	41	15	99	92	42	70	42	15	65	55
292 Crude vegetable materials, n.e.s.	93	71	54	76	26	28	64	90	15	63	58
2 Crude materials, inedible, except fuels	29	44	04	50	42	30	50	16	25	05	30
321 Coal, coke and briquettes	30	06	01	29	90	38	71	06	11	01	28
331 Petroleum, crude and partly refined	94	14	00	03	00	00	00	00	01	01	11
332 Petroleum products	16	65	16	87	63	67	64	29	67	99	57

SITC		38/23	00/00	03/13	33/*	88/65	97/*	22/26	41/00	05/00	61/*	29/76
341	Gas, natural and manufactured											
351	Electric energy											
3	**Mineral fuels, lubricants and related materials**	30	17	27	09	30	29	42	40	03	37	65
411	Animal oils and fats	32	15	14	16	55	64	21	53	43	10	29
421	Fixed vegetable oils, soft	41	03	04	23	45	55	69	81	50	24	53
422	Other fixed vegetable oils	32	00	09	01	23	23	95	62	66	26	12
431	Animal/vegetable oils and fats, processed, and waxes	53	74	72	38	34	64	36	89	30	69	28
4	**Animal and vegetable oils and fats**	37	15	18	20	41	51	54	70	47	22	32
512	Organic chemicals	71	09	86	98	97	57	86	74	85	45	72
513	Inorganic chemicals – elements, oxides, halogen salts	83	69	78	89	84	64	86	99	94	93	78
514	Other inorganic chemicals	64	08	77	95	54	46	64	74	59	62	97
515	Radioactive and associated materials	44	57	80	47	64	55	17	00	08	48	68
521	Crude chemicals from coal, petroleum and gas	52	20	91	02	85	97	86	67	32	46	16
531	Synthetic organic dyestuffs, natural indigo and lakes	49	03	59	30	80	20	57	40	09	92	*
532	Dyeing and tanning extracts, synthetic tanning materials	58	75	78	59	86	27	68	83	94	42	18
533	Pigments, paints, varnishes and related materials	59	82	37	70	68	37	68	66	55	14	53
541	Medicinal and pharmaceutical products	59	50	33	98	72	44	79	31	16	39	23
551	Essential oils, perfume and flavour materials	57	46	98	72	17	60	53	72	46	95	31
553	Perfumery, cosmetics, dentifrices, etc.	47	29	37	53	89	73	60	56	84	64	10
554	Soaps, cleansing and polishing preparations	56	65	32	52	76	48	93	75	74	18	17
561	Fertilisers manufactured	47	02	48	35	61	31	51	88	28	76	83
571	Explosives and pyrotechnic products	50	52	13	74	92	46	14	80	39	62	93
581	Plastic materials, regenerated cellulose and resins	63	13	81	60	80	51	81		53	22	54
599	Chemical materials and products, n.e.s.	61	54	71			52	79			27	
5	**Chemicals**	66	34	68	78	78	54	78	74	97	49	47
611	Leather	72	91	97	81	63	89	89	05	63	76	64
612	Manufacture of leather or of artificial or reconstituted leather	56	27	62	17	71	80	88	98	17	68	28
613	Fur skins, tanned or dressed, including dyed	59	50	93	42	93	92	23	71	22	51	57
621	Materials of rubber	49	12	50	80	84	43	81	64	35	05	32
629	Articles of rubber, n.e.s.	59	14	42	54	55	91	98	88	05	88	56
631	Veneers, plywood boards and other wood, worked, n.e.s.	47	23	05	18	78	91	35	69	61	31	57
632	Wood manufactures, n.e.s.	55	40	17	32	88	91	82	73	03	70	55
633	Cork manufactures	39	00	62	64	68	13	95	14	00	64	11
641	Paper and paperboard	54	17	36	88	76	53	91	84	38	58	34
642	Articles of paper, pulp, paperboard	58	35	50	92	53	65	84	79	26	43	21
651	Textile yarn and thread	53	11	55	37	63	99	89	68	16	85	25
652	Cotton fabrics, woven excl. narrow or special fabrics	55	03	59	94	71	76	72	67	05	87	13
653	Text fabrics woven excl. narrow, special, not cotton	54	11	71	38	25	98	96	72	17	51	07
654	Tulle, lace, embroidery, ribbons, trimmings	55	03	92	92	78	70	51	76	35	94	45
655	Special textile fabrics and related products	65	19	49	94	68	66	96	90	16	99	23
656	Made-up articles, wholly or chiefly of textile materials	55	06	77	62	92	81	75	46	11	96	44
657	Floor coverings, tapestries, etc.	59	06	90	100	98	50	83	26	24	75	99
661	Lime, cement and fabricated building materials – excl. glass/clay materials	63	73	90	09	74	80	08	28	80	61	42
662	Clay and refractory construction materials	57	19	65	42	79	77	89	79	07	77	27
663	Mineral manufactures, n.e.s.	63	27	49	97		67	66	96	81	45	

Table 3.1 (continued)

SITC	Classes	Canada	US	Japan	Belgium–Luxembourg	Netherlands	Germany	France	Italy	UK	Australia	Mean†
664	Glass	01	97	32	27	83	65	72	74	62	14	53
665	Glassware	11	91	28	64	28	67	53	65	84	22	51
666	Pottery	*	07	02	56	68	34	88	93	28	00	42
667	Pearls and precious and semi-precious stones	25	26	90	95	92	79	68	21	95	69	66
671	Pig iron, spiegeleisen, sponge iron, etc.	71	42	03	88	69	85	83	10	40	89	58
672	Ingots and other primary forms of iron or steel	23	68	56	92	63	59	84	26	77	10	56
673	Iron and steel bars, rods, angles, shapes, sections	51	23	10	21	44	66	88	93	78	82	56
674	Universals, plates and sheets of iron or steel	87	42	00	24	81	73	83	92	46	86	61
675	Hoop and strip of iron or steel	*	97	12	16	48	62	97	61	77	30	55
676	Rails and railway track construction materials of iron or steel	19	45	10	18	24	08	35	65	01	79	30
677	Iron and steel wire, excluding wire rod	26	21	05	12	54	48	35	77	24	80	44
678	Tubes, pipes and fittings of iron or steel	36	100	03	89	51	18	63	39	79	59	54
679	Iron steel castings, forgings, unworked, n.e.s.	100	31	67	18	72	42	78	47	26	57	54
681	Silver and platinum group metals	81	52	07	91	56	64	44	17	92	24	53
682	Copper	13	48	25	91	36	75	35	23	59	39	44
683	Nickel	23	34	03	23	64	55	99	10	88	02	40
684	Aluminium	34	90	33	93	91	90	80	60	40	63	67
685	Lead	03	10	34	24	42	92	68	03	57	00	33
686	Zinc	02	24	39	16	89	39	52	03	21	08	29
687	Tin	*	09	01	84	65 *	29	03	04	81	08	31
688	Uranium and thorium and their alloys	*	*	00	00	*	00	00	00	00	00	00
689	Miscellaneous non-ferrous base metals	95	93	82	95	78	42	69	47	68	94	76
691	Finished structural parts and structures, n.e.s.	92	21	08	89	73	57	79	10	26	37	49
692	Metal containers for storage and transport	36	35	14	91	97	50	55	20	44	77	52
693	Wire products – excl. electric – and fencing grills	78	52	05	12	49	46	67	74	44	65	49
694	Nails, screws, nuts, bolts, rivets and similar articles	46	69	11	96	72	38	90	61	80	39	60
695	Tools for use in the hand or in machines	28	54	31	81	75	34	84	84	72	39	58
696	Cutlery	31	48	18	35	80	38	94	99	45	20	51
697	Household equipment of base metals	24	84	21	69	78	44	98	24	77	29	55
698	Manufactures of metal, n.e.s.	31	76	21	79	69	35	99	57	53	54	57
6	Manufactured goods classified chiefly by material	31	57	17	57	33	67	72	52	77	30	49
711	Power generating machinery, other than electric	81	52	90	71	77	43	96	93	45	09	66
712	Agricultural machinery and implements	72	60	71	67	76	36	72	67	23	18	56
714	Office machines	45	48	63	36	92	91	94	66	97	04	64
715	Metal-working machinery	21	75	87	92	57	19	76	90	97	12	63
717	Textile and leather machinery	36	92	35	99	74	28	92	75	60	06	60
718	Machines for special industries	41	29	86	61	86	26	93	83	70	25	60
719	Machinery and appliances – non-electrical – parts	40	32	70	69	74	34	97	69	67	19	57
722	Electric power machinery and switchgear	45	41	46	96	67	45	75	93	63	11	58
723	Equipment for distributing electricity	88	83	12	94	92	34	49	53	29	42	54

724	Telecommunications apparatus	81	94	09	63	91	36	87	75	58	19	61
725	Domestic electrical equipment	29	56	18	25	83	54	69	15	77	54	48
726	Electrical apparatus for medical purposes, radiological apparatus	54	65	83	72	51	35	78	91	34	13	62
729	Other electrical machinery and apparatus	71	53	57	68	81	57	88	86	85	18	66
731	Railway vehicles	90	12	09	59	97	17	25	42	15	44	41
732	Road motor vehicles	89	94	14	97	36	33	64	50	26	32	54
733	Road vehicles other than motor vehicles	24	95	06	84	58	40	71	29	18	12	44
734	Aircraft	96	28	58	60	85	67	64	93	80	02	63
735	Ships and boats	80	38	10	79	50	45	55	65	49	11	48
7	**Machinery and transport equipment**	74	62	36	81	72	39	81	68	57	18	59
812	Sanitary, plumbing, heating and lighting fixtures	34	68	26	90	78	51	79	59	69	60	61
821	Furniture	43	72	19	71	69	62	61	29	86	47	56
831	Travel goods, handbags and similar articles	40	20	16	66	77	67	55	14	76	04	44
841	Clothing except fur clothing	28	43	09	82	53	95	68	15	86	33	49
842	Fur clothing and articles of artificial fur	10	98	50	88	42	75	18	93	75	00	57
851	Footwear	25	06	04	54	80	52	63	01	85	13	38
861	Scientific, medical, optical, meas./contr. instruments	06	54	29	44	79	49	85	91	85	20	54
862	Photographic and cinematographic supplies	19	42	92	25	88	83	99	80	73	40	64
863	Developed cinematographic film	00	38	75	54	36	35	79	52	62	14	45
864	Watches and clocks	17	21	52	22	22	56	90	82	54	02	40
891	Musical instruments, sound recorders and parts	07	85	16	94	90	47	84	62	71	07	60
892	Printed matter	19	54	99	99	69	50	96	60	92	20	64
893	Articles of artificial plastic materials, n.e.s.	17	95	14	96	67	59	90	43	87	31	61
894	Perambulators, toys, games and sporting goods	36	69	26	97	45	81	98	52	69	41	62
895	Office and stationery supplies, n.e.s.	17	54	45	47	71	30	36	69	99	20	52
896	Works of art, collectors' pieces and antiques	69	27	39	90	88	95	63	96	64	25	66
897	Jewellery and gold-/silversmiths' wares	38	87	35	56	33	48	63	07	98	13	47
899	Manufactured articles, n.e.s.	18	52	29	70	62	67	90	62	98	25	57
8	**Miscellaneous manufactured articles**	12	53	26	73	69	61	79	34	84	24	52
911	Postal packages not classified according to kind	*	*	*	00	*	*	00	*	61	00	*
931	Special transactions not classified according to kind	19	49	84	100	84	55	10	00	*	43	54
941	Animals, n.e.s. – incl. zoo animals, dogs and cats	97	68	84	84	*	89	00	50	51	00	50
951	Firearms of war and ammunition therefore	32	09	43	00	*	41	00	70	97	19	34
961	Coin – other than gold, not being legal tender	*	*	00	00	*	20	00	00	87	00	16
9	**Commodities and transactions not classified according to kind**	23	36	84	100	84	54	01	63	73	36	55
	All commodities, unadjusted	48	49	21	63	56	46	65	42	69	17	48
	adjusted	49	52	22	63	61	52	67	45	71	17	50

* Indicates either export or import not available.

† Industry averages in the extreme right column are the unweighted means of individual countries' statistics.

Source: First nine countries: *Commodity Trade: Imports, Exports*, OECD Foreign Trade Statistics, Series C, January–December 1967, Australia: *Commodity Trade Statistics, 1967*, UN Statistical Papers, Series D, vol. XVII.

$$\bar{B}_i = \frac{\Sigma_j \Sigma_i [(X_{ij} + M_{ij}) - |X_{ij} - M_{ij}|]}{\Sigma_j \Sigma_i (X_{ij} + M_{ij})} \tag{3.1}$$

$j = 1, \ldots 10$ are the individual countries. This measure is also the average of the shares of intra-industry trade in each of the countries, weighted by the respective shares of these countries in the total export plus import trade of all ten countries.[2] The weighted average intra-industry trade was 63 per cent in 1967.[3]

These ten countries accounted for 58 per cent of total world exports in 1967, and the average level of intra-industry trade in these countries combined is itself noteworthy. However, this average figure hides many differences among industries and countries, which should be examined.

INTRA-INDUSTRY TRADE BY INDUSTRIES

The columns of Table 3.1 show the percentages of intra-industry trade in each industry of each country. There are also ten rows in the table which show the averages of the 3-digit measures within each of the 1-digit sections, for each of the ten countries. Table 3.2 reproduces the unweighted average across the ten countries of the average level of intra-3-digit trade, for each 1-digit section. The industries are ranked in decreasing order. No industry has an average below 30 per cent. Generally minerals and raw materials have lower percentages than manufactures.

Examination of Table 3.1 shows that there is a considerable variance among the measures for intra-industry trade in the individual 3-digit industries. It is remarkable that there is significant intra-industry trade in every industry. Indeed, only two

[2] We could also compute the weighted average of figures for each industry in place of the unweighted averages in the extreme right column but the additional work is not justified.

[3] Averaging across countries involves some double counting of trade flows since some of the exports (imports) of the individual countries are the imports (exports) of another country within the group of ten. However, this applies to both intra- and inter-industry trade. Furthermore, for our purposes, we need to know the extent to which exports and imports from each country offset each other and it is immaterial whether the export (import) of one country is or is not the import (export) of another country in the group.

TABLE 3.2
Ranking of Industries by Percentage of Intra-Industry Trade

Rank	SITC Class	Description	Percentage
1	5	Chemicals	66
2	7	Machinery and transport equipment	59
3	9	Commodities and transactions, n.e.s.	55
4	8	Miscellaneous manufactured articles	52
5	6	Manufactured goods classified by material	49
6	1	Beverages and tobacco	40
7	4	Animal and vegetable oils and fats	37
8	0	Food and live animals	30
9	2	Crude materials, inedible, except fuels	30
10	3	Mineral fuels, lubricants and related materials	30

industries – 071 (Coffee) and 271 (Crude fertilisers) – had averages below 10 per cent. The prevalence of significant measured intra-industry trade in all industries, primary goods and manufactures, raw materials and semi-processed goods alike, clearly is a phenomenon worth further analysis.

Individual 3-digit industries with percentages over 70 are 099 (Food preparations, n.e.s.), 273 (Stone, sand and gravel), 512 (Organic chemicals), 513 (Inorganic chemicals), 611 (Leather) and 689 (Miscellaneous non-ferrous base metals). The frequency distribution of industry percentages is shown in Fig. 3.1.

Figure 3.1
Distribution of Intra-Industry Shares, by Industry

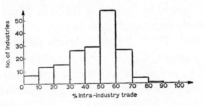

INTRA-INDUSTRY TRADE BY COUNTRIES

Table 3.1 reveals some interesting differences in the percentage of intra-industry trade in individual countries. Table 3.3

presents countries in descending order of the average percentage of intra-industry trade. As can be seen from column 1 of Table 3.3, the UK has the highest average of 69 per cent and is followed closely by France, Belgium–Luxembourg and the Netherlands. The US, Canada, Germany and Italy have $\bar{B}$ values in the forties. Japan and Australia rank lowest with 21 per cent and 17 per cent respectively.

In the remaining five columns of Table 3.3, we show levels and rankings of average values by selected (highest and lowest) 1-digit SITC sections. The rank order of column 1 is duplicated most closely in column 4, representing Manufactures, SITC 6. All the other columns exhibit substantial and apparently non-systematic changes in ranks. The only persistent pattern emerges for Australia and Japan, which stay in ranks 9 and 10 except for once obtaining 8 and 1 each. Japan has a value of 97 per cent in Chemicals. Another notable anomaly is Canada's rank 1 and average value of 65 per cent in Mineral fuels. Closer examination of Canada's SITC 3 shows high values in electric energy (76 per cent) and Petroleum, crude and partly refined (94 per cent).

In the Introduction, we gave a survey of models capable of explaining the phenomenon of intra-industry trade and emphasized the importance of trade in differentiated manufactures. This approach is generally justified by the ranking of industries by SITC sections shown in Table 3.2. For later discussion it is worth noting here the surprisingly high percentages of intra-industry trade in some 3-digit industries of some countries, which do not fall into the category of manufactures. They are mainly raw materials or intermediate products. Values above 90 per cent are found in Canada's trade in Meat, Cheese, Sand, stone and gravel, Iron and steel scrap, and, as already mentioned, Petroleum. The US attains levels above 90 per cent only in Sugar preparations, Crude rubber, Synthetic fibres and Sand, stone and gravel. Japan and Australia have values above 90 per cent only in manufactured food preparations and sugar products. The EEC countries and the UK, on the other hand, have so many industries in the raw materials and semi-manufactures classes with values above 90 per cent that it is too tedious to list them all. Some remarkable, apparently non-differentiated products with high levels of intra-industry trade are Butter for

TABLE 3.3
Intra-Industry Trade, by Country

Country	All Industries B_i	Rank*	Chemicals SITC 5 B_i	Rank	Machinery SITC 7 B_i	Rank	Manufactures SITC 6 B_i	Rank	Crude Materials SITC 2 B_i	Rank	Mineral Fuels SITC 3 B_i	Rank
UK	69	1	68	6	57	7	77	1	25	7	27	7
France	65	2	78	2	81	1	72	2	50	1	30	5
Belgium–Luxembourg	63	3	74	5	81	2	57	4	50	2	40	3
Netherlands	56	4	78	3	72	4	33	7	42	4	42	2
US	49	5	49	8	62	6	57	5	44	3	37	4
Canada	48	6	47	9	74	3	31	8	29	6	65	1
Germany	46	7	54	7	39	8	67	3	30	5	29	6
Italy	42	8	78	4	68	5	52	6	16	8	9	9
Japan	21	9	97	1	36	9	17	10	4	10	3	10
Australia	17	10	34	10	18	10	30	9	5	9	17	8

* In case of a tie the rank is based on that of all industries.

Germany (97 per cent), Meal and flour for the Netherlands (96 per cent), Fresh vegetables for Belgium (94 per cent) and Australia (98 per cent), Cocoa for the Netherlands (96 per cent), Hides and skins for the Netherlands (98 per cent), Sand, stone and gravel for all countries, Iron ore and concentrates for France (92 per cent), Coal, coke and briquettes for the Netherlands (90 per cent), Gas for Germany (97 per cent), France (88 per cent) and Petroleum products for Australia (99 per cent). This last item is the subject of a case study in Chapter 4.

It is recalled from Chapter 2 that a country's trade imbalance introduces a downward bias into the measure of intra-industry trade, which can be eliminated by an appropriate adjustment. The last two rows of Table 3.1 show the $\bar{B}_i$ and $\bar{C}_i$ values of each country. $\bar{C}_i$ is larger than or equal to $\bar{B}_i$ in all cases, as predicted. The excess of the adjusted ($\bar{C}_i$) values over the unadjusted ($\bar{B}_i$) values averages 2·3 points, or about 5 per cent of $\bar{B}_i$. In the cases of the Netherlands and Germany, which had large trade surpluses in 1967, the adjustments amount to about 9 and 13 per cent respectively. This analysis implies that the intra-industry trade values for individual industries presented in Table 3.1 and analysed above might well be higher by an average of 5 per cent if trade of these countries had been in overall balance during the year 1967, and commodity distribution of exports and imports was unchanged.

TRENDS IN INTRA-INDUSTRY TRADE IN OECD
COUNTRIES: 1959–67

In the appendix we have reproduced tables of the percentage of intra-industry trade for 1959 and 1964, which are identical in design to Table 3.1 but there are some inconsistencies in the coverage of the data, as noted in the appendix tables. However, for the present purpose of analysing the general trend in intra-industry trade through time, we are concerned with summary statistics whose comparability over time is affected only marginally by differences in the coverage of some 3-digit industries among the three years. Thus we have observations for three different years spanning a period of eight years.

Before engaging in an analysis of our intra-industry trade measures it is useful to recall some characteristics of the period

1959–67 covered in this study. We chose the starting year 1959 because it marked the return to currency convertibility by the major countries of Western Europe, and the beginning of the trade liberalisation among members of the EEC. The terminal year of our inquiry, 1967, was imposed on us by data avail-ability. However, it turns out to have been a relatively normal year in comparison with the last years of the sixties, and the early seventies, when the Vietnam war and world-wide inflation changed trade patterns and resulted in the imposition of artificial barriers to trade and capital flow especially by the US and the UK.

The period 1959–67 was characterised by a rapid growth in the value of world trade and trade of the countries in the sample. The trade of this group of countries grew from $125 billion in 1959 to $250 billion in 1967, an average compound rate of growth of 9 per cent per annum. During this period two significant sets of trade liberalisation measures were carried out. First, the EEC and EFTA countries lowered internal tariffs towards zero at a rapid pace. Second, the Kennedy Round of tariff reductions lowered tariffs among all industrial countries of the world. These developments are important because trade liberalisation and the Heckscher–Ohlin model under its normal set of assumptions, as discussed in Chapter 1, imply an increased tendency towards national specialisation. If, therefore, we find increased intra-industry trade during this period, our case for a thorough re-examination of the assumptions of the traditional Heckscher–Ohlin model is strengthened.

In Tables 3.4 and 3.5 we present the most important summary statistics of the percentages of intra-industry trade for the three years, by industries and countries respectively. Starting with the global averages shown in the last rows of the two tables, we can see that intra-industry trade as a percentage of total trade rose steadily from 36 per cent in 1959 to 42 per cent in 1964 and 48 per cent in 1967, or by 17 per cent in the five-year period 1959–64 and 33 per cent in the nine-year period 1959–67.[4]

The increase in intra-industry trade of all ten countries com-bined can also be compared with the increase in total export

[4] We have no evidence of the trend since then except for Australia. The adjusted global average for Australia in 1968–9 was 20 per cent compared to 17 per cent in 1967.

TABLE 3.4

Changes in Intra-Industry Trade, by Industry

SITC	Levels			Absolute Change		Percentage Change	
	1959	1964	1967	1959–64	1959–67	1959–64	1959–67
0 Food and live animals	22	25	30	3	8	13·6	36·3
1 Beverages and tobacco	40	42	40	2	0	5·0	0·0
2 Crude material	26	28	30	2	4	7·7	15·4
3 Mineral fuels	30	29	30	−1	0	−3·3	0·0
4 Oils and fats	41	39	37	−2	−4	−5·0	−10·0
5 Chemicals	56	60	66	4	8	7·1	14·2
6 Manufactures	43	49	49	6	6	13·9	13·9
7 Machinery	43	53	59	10	16	23·3	37·2
8 Miscellaneous manufacturing	45	53	52	8	7	17·7	15·5
9 Commodity, n.e.s.	34	45	55	11	21	32·4	61·8
Mean	36	42	48	6	12	16·7	33·3

TABLE 3.5

Changes in Intra-Industry Trade, by Country

Countries	Levels			Absolute Change		Percentage Change	
	1959	1964	1967	1959–64	1959–67	1959–64	1959–67
Canada	28	35	48	7	20	25·0	71·4
US	40	40	49	0	9	0·0	22·5
Japan	17	21	21	4	4	23·5	23·5
Belgium–Luxembourg	53	60	63	7	10	13·0	18·9
Netherlands	55	58	56	3	1	5·5	1·9
Germany	39	42	46	3	7	7·9	17·9
France	45	60	65	5	20	11·1	44·4
Italy	35	44	42	9	7	25·7	20·0
UK	32	40	69	8	37	25·0	115·6
Australia	14	17	17	3	3	21·4	21·4
Mean	36	42	48	6	12	16·7	33·3

plus import trade of these countries. We find that the 1959–67 increase in intra-industry trade ($153 billion) accounted for 80 per cent of the total increase in export plus import trade ($191 billion).

In Table 3.6 the trends in intra-industry trade are shown in terms of two more traditional quantities, 'net' trade ($X_i - M_i$)

and total trade $(X_i + M_i)$. Net trade is the same as the 'inter-industry trade' of Chapter 2. We have calculated the percentage changes of total and net trade for all industries during the period 1959–67. Table 3.6 shows separately the percentage changes for all trade by country and, for all countries combined, the changes in trade by individual industry, on the left and right panels respectively. Total trade grew over three times as rapidly

TABLE 3.6
Growth in Net and Total Trade during 1959–67 (%)

All Trade	Countries		All Countries (SITC)	Industries	
	Net Trade	Total Trade		Net Trade	Total Trade
Canada	−10	91	0	92	72
US	−84	85	1	72	68
Japan	205	219	2	44	49
Belgium–Luxembourg	77	127	3	20	80
Netherlands	82	92	4	36	23
Germany	97	125	5	92	122
France	46	128	6	156	325
Italy	165	182	7	103	202
UK	118	379	8	113	149
Australia	75	81	9	143	180
Total	50	159	*Total*	50	159

as net trade, that is, 50 per cent compared to 159 per cent, which is another way of reporting that intra-industry trade levels increased. However, the growth of net trade shows more clearly than the growth of intra-industry trade why estimates of income and price elasticities and tests of comparative advantage which use net exports or imports are biased.

There are some notable differences among countries in their relative growth rates for net and total trade. In all countries total trade grew more rapidly than net trade. Canada and the US showed positive growth rates for total trade but negative rates for net trade. Japan's total and net trade grew by almost equal percentages. The UK showed the highest growth rate of total trade but only the third highest rate for net trade. A linear regression showed no significant relationship between increases in net and total trade ($R^2 = 0\cdot12$) or between increases in total trade and $\bar{B}$-values ($R^2 = 0\cdot02$).

The rise in trade classified by industries shows that the largest increases in total trade took place in SITC 6 and 7, Manufactures (325 per cent) and Machinery (202 per cent) respectively. The smallest increases were experienced by SITC 4 and 2, Oils and fats (23 per cent) and Crude materials (49 per cent) respectively. The growth in net trade was smaller than that in gross trade in all SITC classes, except 0, 1 and 4. A high and statistically significant linear regression was found between net and total trade increase across industries ($R^2 = 0\cdot71$) but not between total trade and the $\bar{B}$ values.

Turning now to an examination of the changes in intra-industry trade measures for industries shown in Table 3.4, the greatest percentage gain of 62 per cent over the entire period was in the quantitatively unimportant SITC Section 9, Commodities, n.e.s. The second highest average gain of 37 per cent took place in SITC Class 7, Machinery and transport equipment. One quantitatively important industry in this group is automobiles (732) which had B values of 31 per cent, 42 per cent and 54 per cent in the years 1959, 1964 and 1967 respectively. The strength of intra-industry trade in Mineral fuels stayed unchanged during 1959–67 after falling slightly during the earlier subperiod. The only reduction in the percentage of intra-industry trade occurred in the SITC 4, Animal and vegetable oils and fats. A trend persisting throughout the period reduced the value by 10 per cent over the nine years.

Table 3.5 reveals that the intra-industry trade of all countries rose during the full period being considered. The most dramatic gains were made by the UK and Canada with percentage increases of 116 and 71 respectively, for the period 1959–67. The increase for the Netherlands of only 1·9 per cent over this period was by far the smallest of all countries. During the subperiod 1964–7 the Netherlands and Italy experienced decreases, and Japan and Australia no changes in the average levels. A fact worth noting because of our preceding reference to the trade liberalisation measures of the EEC is that the unweighted average increases in the intra-industry trade measures for the

EEC countries were 12·6 per cent and 20·6 per cent during the periods 1959–64 and 1959–67 respectively. Both these increases were below the average for all of the countries in the sample.

INTRA-INDUSTRY TRADE IN OTHER COUNTRIES

The preceding statistics of the intra-industry trade phenomena were for a sample of ten industrialised nations, whose international trade is concentrated in finished and semi-finished manufactures where product differentiation and narrow specialisation are strongest. In contrast the trade of developing countries is concentrated much more heavily in raw materials, semi-manufactures and other staples providing relatively little opportunity for product differentiation. Moreover, in these countries, manufacturing sectors are small and competition through product differentiation, which is so prevalent in the developed countries, is much less. In the remaining part of this chapter, we will present and analyse, briefly, empirical evidence on the magnitude of intra-industry trade in Yugoslavia and south-east Asian countries.[5]

Intra-industry trade of Yugoslavia is of special interest since the country is not only developing but also subject to a very high degree of central direction. Presumably this kind of central direction by planners would want to avoid the disadvantages of monopolistic competition through product differentiation in consumer goods, by limiting both imported substitutes for domestic products and the production of smaller numbers of substitutes for domestic consumption and export. This kind of development strategy is advocated by many critics of the free market system. In practice it is constrained by the value that consumers attach to what appears to others as frivolous differentiation and by the realities of economies of scale in the production of substitutes discussed in Chapter 1. For these reasons it is of some interest to measure the extent to which intra-industry trade prevails in a country where ideology should diminish the influence of one of its main causes, product differentiation.

[5] The share of intra-industry trade in the total trade among Central American Common Market countries is reviewed in Chapter 9.

Table A3.3 contains the percentages of Yugoslav external trade which is intra-industry trade at the 2-digit SITC level of aggregation computed by Vukasovich (1970) for the years 1961, 1964 and 1968. The share of intra-2-digit trade is over 30 per cent for most of the 2-digit industries, and the average for all Yugoslav trade increased substantially from 47 per cent in 1961 and 48 per cent in 1964 to 63 per cent in 1968. Unfortunately the absolute levels of these shares cannot be compared directly with those of the OECD countries because of the differences in the levels of aggregation.[6] However, in Chapter 4, we reproduce comparable 2-digit shares of intra-industry trade for Australia. The global adjusted average for Australia at the 2-digit level was 25·9 per cent in 1968–9. This is much less than the Yugoslav percentage. Moreover, at least in the case of Australia, the 2-digit shares are not much greater than the 3-digit average which was 20·2 per cent for the same year. It appears, therefore, that the Yugoslav average intra-industry trade is high relative to that of the developed OECD countries.

Table A3.4 reproduces the measures of intra-industry trade for south-east Asia which have been computed by Hesketh (1973) for the year 1962. The computations were restricted to the manufacturing industries within Sections 5–8 of the SITC. The main finding is that for all the developing countries individually the average intra-2-digit trade is less than 20 per cent. The south-east Asian country figures are generally much less than the averages of the 3-digit figures within the manufacturing Sections 5–8 for the OECD countries which are given in Tables A3.1 and A3.2 for the years 1964 and 1959 respectively and which must be less than the corresponding 2-digit averages. They are also much less than the corresponding 2-digit figures for Yugoslavia in Table A3.3. Moreover, the south-east Asian figures are very much less than the comparable 2-digit figures for Japan and Australia which Hesketh calculated.

[6] In Chapter 9 we report measures of intra-industry trade at the 2-digit level for intra-EEC trade of the members of EEC. The mean for intra-industry trade share within the EEC was 66 per cent in 1967, or 70 per cent if the country averages are adjusted. As the global shares for each country are equivalent to weighted averages of the intra-industry trade share of bilateral trade, the 2-digit share of intra-industry trade with all trading partners could be greater or less than the average share with EEC partners alone.

SUMMARY AND CONCLUSIONS

The objective of this chapter is to demonstrate the empirical significance of intra-industry trade in order to justify the theoretical models developed in Part II. It is difficult to know whether we have succeeded in our demonstration. The concept of intra-industry trade and its statistical measurement are new to most economists and there is nothing which could readily be used as an objective standard by which to judge the case.

It is obvious from this book that we are convinced that these data reveal an empirical phenomenon deserving more attention than it has received in the past. The levels of intra-industry trade among developed, developing, highly protected and directed economies that we have shown to exist stand in support of this judgement. In the next chapter, we will provide some additional evidence about the magnitude of intra-industry trade through the analysis of intra-industry percentages as a function of aggregation levels, from 7 to 1 digits, for Australia's trade in the year 1968–9. We hope to demonstrate through this case study that the observed intra-industry trade is not mainly due to the use of trade data at too high a level of aggregation.

4 The Aggregation Question – A Case Study of Australian Data

The analysis of aggregation and its effect on measured intra-industry trade to be presented in this chapter is based on Australian trade data for the year 1968–9. We chose Australia for this study because of the availability of the data in convenient form on an electronic tape.[1] The tapes of Australian commodity exports and imports for 1968–9 recorded the values

[1] In addition to the enormous computational advantages, the tape has the advantage over official printed statistics in that all flows under $500 are lumped together under item number 999.99.99 in the printed statistics whereas they are recorded under the proper numbers on the tape. It should be noted that the Australian export figures employed include re-exports. Australian commodity trade statistics are based on the SITC. Both exports and imports are valued f.o.b.

There are two sources of error with this data although, fortunately, both are minor. First, there are differences between the Australian Import Commodity Classification and the Australian Export Commodity Classification at the 7-digit and the 5-digit levels. At the 7-digit and 5-digit levels there are some import items with no corresponding item in the export classification and some items with matching descriptions but different numbers. The larger number of import items will tend to bias downwards the measures of intra-commodity trade at this level of aggregation but since those SITC items which are not listed in the export classification are those for which there are no significant Australian exports the bias is small.

The second problem is that the records of some 46 out of approximately 2000 7-digit export items and some 32 out of an even larger number of import items have been deleted because they are confidential. The total value of trade deleted is $89 million, which is 1·3 per cent of total export plus import trade. Fortunately these exclusions are spread fairly widely throughout the sections of the import and export classifications and as exclusion may bias a measure either downwards or upwards the effect of these exclusions on the global averages for trade with individual countries or with all countries combined is negligible. These exclusions may have biased slightly some of the individual commodity measures at the 5- and, in a very few cases, at the 3-digit level.

of trade in commodities at the 7-digit level. These data were used to compute intra-industry for all industries at the 7-, 5-, 3-, 2- and 1-digit levels. The disadvantages associated with a study of Australia are that it is a semi-industrialised country and that its manufacturing industry is highly protected by transport costs and tariffs. Consequently, Australia's intra-industry trade at the 3-digit level of the SITC was 17 per cent of its total commodity trade in 1967 whereas the unweighted average for ten major industrial countries was 50 per cent at that time (see Table 3.1). In some ways, therefore, the results of the analysis are not representative. On the other hand, the high levels of intra-industry trade for some Australian industries indicate that the phenomenon of intra-industry trade is not restricted to trade among highly industrialised countries but exists even in the trade of nations which are more specialised in the production and export of agricultural and mining products and which have high levels of protection for their manufacturing industries.

AGGREGATION AND MEASURED INTRA-INDUSTRY TRADE

Table 4.1 gives the averages of Australian intra-industry trade, adjusted and unadjusted (in parentheses), for all industries as a percentage of its trade with major trading partners and of its total trade. Consider, first, Australian trade with all other countries combined. As can be seen (last row), at the most detailed 7-digit level of classification, intra-industry trade represents an average of 6·2 per cent of total trade with all partners. It is difficult to judge whether this percentage of intra-industry trade is important since there is no ready standard of comparison. However, it is important to note that the SITC classification is not sufficiently sensitive, even at the 7-digit level, to discriminate among the forms of differentiation which give rise to the simultaneous import and export of the 'industry's' output.

Measured intra-industry trade rises rapidly as the degree of aggregation increases, reaching 20 per cent at the most widely used 3-digit levels and 43 per cent at the 1-digit levels. As noted above, this increase in the measure depends on the extent to

TABLE 4.1
*Australian Intra-Industry Trade with Major Trading Partners at
Different Levels of Aggregation, 1968–9*

Country or Country Group	Digit Level of Aggregation				
	7	5	3	2	1
US	3·2	10·0	14·6	25·0	39·7
	(2·3)	(7·0)	(10·3)	(17·5)	(27·8)
UK	1·3	4·2	7·7	12·5	31·5
	(1·0)	(3·1)	(5·7)	(9·3)	(23·5)
Japan	0·2	2·2	4·8	10·6	18·0
	(0·2)	(1·5)	(3·3)	(7·2)	(12·2)
EEC	1·0	3·2	4·9	6·3	15·3
	(1·0)	(3·2)	(4·9)	(6·3)	(15·3)
Canada	0·8	7·2	17·6	27·5	38·6
	(0·4)	(4·1)	(10·0)	(15·7)	(22·0)
New Zealand	4·4	19·5	30·5	47·5	79·8
	(2·8)	(12·3)	(19·3)	(30·1)	(50·5)
Hong Kong	1·4	6·5	13·3	17·3	50·5
	(1·1)	(5·0)	(10·3)	(13·4)	(39·1)
India	0·2	1·8	5·5	9·5	49·5
	(0·2)	(17·8)	(5·5)	(9·5)	(49·5)
South Africa	0·7	7·3	16·3	30·3	65·4
	(0·4)	(4·5)	(10·0)	(18·7)	(40·3)
South-east Asia	1·5	4·4	8·7	9·8	17·4
	(1·0)	(3·0)	(5·9)	(6·6)	(11·7)
Rest of the world	3·1	10·6	18·9	27·0	52·0
	(3·0)	(10·3)	(18·3)	(26·1)	(50·3)
All countries	6·2	14·9	20·2	25·9	42·9
	(6·1)	(14·6)	(19·7)	(25·3)	(42·0)

Notes
1 The statistics are global averages for all SITC sections. In each case the first row of figures is adjusted for global bilateral trade imbalances; the figures in parentheses are unadjusted.
2 Countries are ranked in decreasing order of the value of exports to Australia in 1968–9, except for the remainder groups of south-east Asia and the rest of the world. South-east Asia consists of Brunei, Cambodia, Laos, Malaysia, Indonesia, Philippines, Singapore, Thailand and the Republic of Vietnam.

which the differences between exports and imports of the sub-industries are of different sign.[2] It is quite possible for a low level of intra-commodity trade among several 'industries', reflecting the fact that the country exports and does not import the products of some of these industries while it imports and does not export the others, to become a high level of intra-industry trade when these industries are aggregated. We examined the data to assess the significance of these changes by calculating the averages of the 3-digit measures within each of the 2-digit items and the averages of the 5-digit measures within each of the 3-digit items. The simple correlation coefficients between the 2-digit measures and the corresponding 3-digit averages and between the 3-digit measures and the corresponding 5-digit averages are 0·905 and 0·705 respectively. This demonstrates that over the 2-, 3- and 5-digit levels of aggregation the patterns of intra-commodity trade are essentially preserved when the data are aggregated from 5-digit to 3-digit and to 2-digit items. This result implies that industries preserve their relative strength of intra-industry trade through these levels of aggregation, and studies of differences among industries would be insensitive to the level of aggregation chosen.

These results are confirmed by Table 4.2 which lists the industries, and a brief description of each, which had averages for Australian trade with all countries of over 75 per cent in 1968–9 at the 3-, 5- and 7-digit levels of aggregation. This tabulation shows clearly that high levels of intra-industry trade persist at all levels of aggregation.

The same general conclusions concerning the effects of aggregation apply to Australia's trade with individual trading partners. In particular the industries which show high levels of intra-industry trade at one level of aggregation generally have sub-industries at a more disaggregated level which have high levels of intra-industry trade. The correspondences between industries at the 3-digit and 5-digit levels of aggregation of

---

[2] It is worth recalling that the variance of the components of an aggregate does not determine the effects of aggregation. The components may have a wide variance and, yet, aggregating these components will not change the average level of intra-commodity trade if exports exceed imports in all components, or vice versa. This sometimes occurs in the Australian statistics.

Australian trade with New Zealand which have high levels of intra-industry trade were reported in Lloyd (1971, Table A3). It is remarkable that the percentage of intra-industry trade is highest with New Zealand and South Africa, which are countries with resource endowments and levels of development similar to those of Australia. We return to the analysis of Australia–New Zealand trade in Chapter 9. We may also note in passing the surprising result that intra-industry trade with the EEC and south-east Asia are at almost identical levels.

One important aspect of the distribution of these measures at each level of aggregation that is worth considering separately is the number of the industries which have high, measured intra-industry trade. Table 4.2 reveals that although the index *averages* increase with aggregation, the *number* of individual industries with very high levels decrease with aggregation. There are 13 industries above 75 per cent at the 3-digit level, 74 at the 5-digit level and 135 at the 7-digit level. The last number is perhaps the most surprising since the large number of non-matching numbers in the export and import classifications at this level must have seriously biased these measures downwards (see footnote 1, p. 48).

A careful study of the SITC classification, and the results of the calculations already presented, has convinced us that the 3-digit SITC statistics separate commodities into groups most closely corresponding to the concept of an 'industry' used conventionally in economic analysis. (One exception is the iron and steel industry, for which the 2-digit level (67) appears to be more appropriate.) As further evidence that intra-industry trade measured at this level is an economic meaningful phenomenon we give a preliminary, impressionistic analysis of the pattern of intra-industry trade for a few selected industries in Australia. We discuss some more rigorous empirical tests of the determinants tests of intra-industry trade in Chapter 11.

EXAMPLES OF INTRA-INDUSTRY TRADE

Examining the 3-digit industries shown in Table 4.2 which have over 75 per cent intra-industry trade, there are a few instances for which the causes of the simultaneous exports and imports require little theorising once the precise nature of the goods in

TABLE 4.2

Intra-Industry Trade above 75 per cent from 5-, 3- and 2-Digit SITC Statistics of Australian Trade, 1968–9

Digit level of aggregation

5	3	2
Section 0: Food and live animals		
03202 Prepared or preserved crustaceans and molluscs		03 Fish and fish preparations
04812 Prepared foods obtained by swelling or roasting cereal grains		
04830 Macaroni, spaghetti, noodles, vermicelli and similar products		
05350 Fruit and vegetable juices, unfermented		
05551 Vegetable and fruit preserved with vinegar	054 Vegetables, fresh, frozen or simply preserved	
06202 Flavoured or coloured sugars and syrups and molasses		
07130 Coffee extracts, essences, concentrates		
07300 Chocolate and other cocoa food preparations	073 Chocolate and other cocoa food preparations	
08140 Flours and meals of meat or fish	081 Feeding-stuff for animals	08 Feeding-stuff for animals
09907 Vinegar and substitutes for vinegar	099 Food preparations, n.e.s.	09 Miscellaneous preparations chiefly for food

Table 4.2 (*continued*)

5	3	2
Section 2: Crude materials, inedible (except fuels)		
21200 Fur skins, undressed	212 Fur skins, undressed	
22150 Linseed		
22190 Flour and meal of oil-seeds		
26320 Cotton linters		
26640 Synthetic and man-made fibres, waste		29 Crude animal and vegetable materials, n.e.s.
	273 Stone, sand and gravel	
Section 3: Mineral fuels, lubricants and related materials		
33220 Kerosene, jet fuel, white spirit and other refined burning oils		
33230 Distillate fuels	332 Petroleum products	
33240 Residual fuel oils		
33292 Pitch from coal tar		
33295 Bitumen and other petroleum residues		
Section 4: Animal and vegetable oils and fats		
41110 Oils and fats of fish and marine mammals		
43131 Fatty acids		
Section 5: Chemicals		51 Chemical elements and compounds

61 Leather, n.e.s., and dressed fur skins

67 Iron and steel

533 Pigments, paints, varnishes and related materials

611 Leather

674 Universals, plates and sheets of iron or steel

677 Iron and steel wire (except wire rod)

53331 Prepared pigments, enamels, glazes

54163 Bacterial products, anti-sera, vaccines
55430 Polishes, pastes, powder and similar preparations
57121 Mining, blasting and safety fuses
58191 Hardened proteins (e.g. casein and gelatin)
59955 Gelatin and gelatin derivatives
59994 Preparations for soldering, brazing or welding

Section 6: Manufactured goods classified chiefly by materials

61220 Saddlery, and other harness-makers' goods
63240 Builders' woodwork and prefabricated wood buildings
64211 Paper boxes, bags and other packing containers
64220 Writing blocks, envelopes
66110 Quicklime, slaked lime and hydraulic lime
66320 Natural or artificial abrasive powder or grain
67312 Wire rod of high-carbon steel
67343 Angles, shapes and sections
67421 Untinned plates and sheets

67432 Uncoated plates and sheets
67701 Iron and steel wire of solid section

67702 Wire of high-carbon steel
68213 Copper master alloys, n.e.s.

Table 4.2 (*continued*)

5	3	2
68410 Unworked aluminium and aluminium alloys	684 Aluminium and aluminium alloys	
68422 Aluminium plates, sheets and strip		
68425 Aluminium tubes, pipes, blanks		
68524 Lead tubes, pipes and blanks		
68950 Cadmium and other base metals and their alloys, n.e.s.	689 Miscellaneous non-ferrous base metals and their alloys	
69212 Copper tanks, vats and reservoirs		
69232 Aluminium compressed gas cylinders and containers		
69312 Copper stranded wire, cables and the like		
69313 Aluminium stranded wire, cables and the like		
69331 Iron and steel gauze, cloth, netting		
69422 Copper nuts, bolts, screws and the like		
69711 Iron and steel household non-electric cooking and heating appliances		
69894 Articles of aluminium, n.e.s.		
Section 7: Machinery and transport equipment		
71523 Gas-operated welding, brazing and cutting appliances		
71839 Other non-domestic food-processing machines, non-electric		
71915 Refrigerators and equipment non-domestic and non-electric		

72505	Electric water and immersion heaters	
72912	Electric batteries	
73220	Public service passenger vehicles (motor-buses, coaches, etc.)	

Section 8: Miscellaneous manufactured goods

81220	Ceramic sinks, wash basins and other sanitary fixtures	
85105	Gaiters, leggings, cricket pads and similar articles	
86121	Frames and mountings for spectacles and the like	
86161	Projectors, enlargers and reducers (except cinematographic)	
86198	Instruments and apparatus for physical or chemical analysis	94 Animals, n.e.s. (including zoo animals, dogs and cats)
89410	Baby and invalid carriages and parts	
89424	Equipment for table and fun-fair games	
89595	Sealing-wax – copying paste	
89601	Works of art – paintings, drawings and pastels	
89932	Matches	
89933	Combustible materials and preparations, n.e.s.	
89996	Fans and hand screens, non-mechanical	941 Animals, n.e.s. (including zoo animals, dogs and cats)

Section 9: Other merchandise

| 94100 | Animals, n.e.s. (including zoo animals, dogs and cats) | 94100 Animals, n.e.s. (including zoo animals, dogs and cats) |

the subclasses is realised. Thus, trade in Group 941, which consists principally of zoo animals and pet dogs and cats, is based on absolute national advantage or purely historical factors. Similarly, in Group 212 (Fur skins, undressed) Australia exported kangaroo and wallaby skins worth $1·2 million and rabbit skins worth a little over half a million dollars and imported mink worth $0·8 million. This is an example of distinctly different products in the one aggregate.

Different causes are responsible for the two observed high levels of intra-industry trade in important Australian industries, Iron and steel goods (SITC 67) and Petroleum products (SITC 332). Table 4.3 shows the absolute levels of exports and imports and intra-industry measures for the 3-digit and the important 5-digit industries of the iron and steel industry. As can be seen, intra-industry trade is high for all of the 3-digit industries, except 671 and 672, and for most of the 5-digit industries. The results for industry 671 should be disregarded since, for reasons of confidentiality, most exports in the group were deleted from the records.

A study of the descriptions of the 5-digit industries reveals that they leave much room for the inclusion of similar products differentiated in apparently minor ways. But it must be these minor product differences which give rise to the trade. The basic explanation for this pattern of exports and imports of iron and steel products is that Australia is an efficient producer of some, but not all, the finely differentiated products of this industry. Australian producers of iron and steel goods have ready access to abundant supplies of high-grade iron-ore deposits and coal, conveniently located near tidewater and both of which are now exported on a substantial scale. Thus Australia's source of comparative advantage or disadvantage must be found in costs specific to individual, narrow product lines. While we have not been able to estimate the importance of these sources of economies of scale in the case of Australia's iron and steel industry, the existence of such economies in narrow product lines is sufficient to explain the observed intra-industry trade. They are also consistent with the findings of the Australian Tariff Board which studied part of the industry: 'Comparisons which could be made of British and local unit costs suggest that local manufacturers are at an advantage in producing some

TABLE 4.3

Intra-Industry Trade in Iron and Steel Goods (Division 67), 1968–9

SITC item	Brief description	Exports ($'000)	Imports ($'000)	5-digit measure and av.‡ measure	3-digit measure
671	Pig iron, spiegeleisen, sponge iron, etc. and ferro-alloys	151*†	6,339†	3·5	4·6
672	Ingots and other primary forms of iron and steel	31,656†	1,116†	0·2	6·8
67311	Wire rod of iron or steel (except high-carbon or alloy steel)	8,136	363	8·0	
67312	Wire rod of high-carbon steel	20	15	86·0	
67313	Wire rod of alloy steel	11	1,038	2·0	
67321	Bars and rods (except wire rod)	5,074	1,575	47·4	
67322	Bars and rods (except wire rod) of high-carbon steel	269	627	60·1	
67323	Bars and rods (except wire rod) of alloy steel	398	5,286	14·0	
67341	Angles, shapes and sections, 80 mm or more (except of high-carbon or alloy steel)	5,064	1,751	51·4	
67342	Angles, shapes and sections, 80 mm or more of high-carbon steel	17	5	44·9	
67343	Angles, shapes and sections, 80 mm or more of alloy steel	69	88	88·1	
67351	Angles, shapes and sections, less than 80 mm (except of high-carbon or alloy steel)	2,051	403	32·9	
67352	Angles, shapes and sections, less than 80 mm of high-carbon steel	33	20	74·1	
67353	Angles, shapes and sections, less than 80 mm of alloy steel	33	59	71·8	
673	Iron and steel bars, rods, angles, shapes and sections	21,797	11,230	29·7	68·0
67411	Untinned plates and sheets more than 4·75 mm thick (except of high-carbon or alloy steel)	4,548	1,281	43·9	

Table 4.3 (*continued*)

SITC item	Brief description	Exports ($'000)	Imports ($'000)	5-digit measure and av.‡ measure	3-digit measure
67412	Universals, plates and sheets, more than 4·75 mm thick, of high-carbon steel	24	57	59·6	
67413	Universals, plates and sheets, more than 4·75 mm thick, of alloy steel	72	2,391	5·9	
67414	Universals (except of high-carbon or alloy steel)	73	7	18·0	
67421	Untinned plates and sheets, 3 to 4·75 mm thick (except of high-carbon or alloy steel)	8,001	6,859	92·3	
67422	Plates and sheets, 3 to 4·75 mm thick, of high-carbon steel	1	24	8·9	
67423	Plates and sheets, 3 to 4·75 mm thick, of alloy steel	71	726	17·7	
67431	Uncoated plates and sheets less than 3 mm thick (except of high-carbon or alloy steel)	2,064	10,986	31·6	
67432	Uncoated plates and sheets less than 3 mm thick of high-carbon steel	37	50	85·4	
67433	Uncoated plates and sheets less than 3 mm thick of alloy steel	82	5,156	3·1	
67470	Tinned plates and sheets (except of high-carbon or alloy steel)	5,424	546	18·3	
67481	Coated plates and sheets less than 3 mm thick (except of high-carbon or alloy steel)	15,784	1,941	21·9	
67482	Coated plates and sheets less than 3 mm thick of high-carbon steel	1	0	0·0	
67483	Coated plates and sheets less than 3 mm thick of alloy steel	3	2,573	0·3	
674	Universals, plates and sheets of iron and steel	28,984	26,424	24·6	95·4
675	Hoop and strip of iron or steel	1,952	7,163	42·8	42·8
676	Railway and tramway track construction material	653	286	23·5	60·8

677	Iron and steel wire (except wire rod)	3,070	3,948	69·7	87·5
678	Tubes, pipes and fittings of iron or steel	8,041	39,114	32·8	34·1
679	Iron and steel castings and forgings, unworked, n.e.s.	992	227	37·3	37·3

* Exports of spiegeleisen (671.10.00) and pig iron and cast iron (671.20.00) have been excluded as they are confidential.
† Some of the five-digit items in 671 and 672 do not match because of differences in the Australian export and import commodity classifications at this level.
‡ The averages in column 5 are the weighted averages of all 5-digit items in the respective 3-digit commodities.

TABLE 4.4

Intra-Industry Trade in Petroleum and Petroleum Products, 1968–9

SITC item	Brief description	Exports ($'000)	Imports ($'000)	Measure
Group 331	Petroleum, crude and partly refined (excluding natural gasoline)	11	214,244	0·0
331.01	Crude petroleum	0	174,791	0·0
331.02	Petroleum, partly refined	11	39,453	0·1
Group 332	Petroleum products	26,414	36,941	83·4
332.10	Motor spirit (automotive and aviation)	6,919	13,457	67·9
332.10.01	Automotive spirit	6,469	8,173	88·4
332.10.02	Aviation gasoline	47	20,070	4·5
332.10.09	Other petroleum spirits	402	3,214	22·3
332.20	Kerosene, jet fuel, white spirit and refined burning oils	2,893	3,310	93·3
332.20.01	White spirit	522	193	54·1
332.20.02	Aviation kerosene (aviation turbine fuel)	2,146	1,791	91·0
332.20.03	Power kerosene	10	283	6·9
332.20.09	Lighting kerosene and other light, heating and burning oils, n.e.i.	216	1,042	34·3
332.30	Distillate fuels	4,234	4,336	98·8
332.30.02	Automotive distillate (diesel oils)	3,750	3,757	99·9
332.30.05	Industrial and marine diesel fuel	433	579	85·6
332.30.09	Heavy distillates, n.e.i.	51	0	0·0
332.40	Residual fuel oils	4,012	5,668	82·9
332.40.01	Furnace fuel (including ships' bunker fuel)	} 4,012	5,668	} 82·9
332.40.09	Other		0	

Code	Description			
332.51	Lubricating preparations (at least 70% by weight petroleum products)	} 7,811	3,668	} 76·1
332.52	Lubricating preparations (less than 70% by weight petroleum products)		1,133	
332.61	Petroleum jelly	12	184	11·9
332.62	Mineral waxes	84	1,592	10·0
332.91	Non-lubricating oils	71	1,264	10·6
332.92	Pitch from coal or other mineral tars	52	51	98·5
332.93	Pitch coke	0	0	0·0
332.94	Petroleum, coke	0	2,025	0·0
332.95	Petroleum, bitumen and other shale-oil residuals	86	124	82·3
332.96	Asphalt, mastic and other bituminous mixtures	239	129	70·1
Group 341	Petroleum gases and other gaseous hydrocarbons	112	31	43·6

types of tube but that in other cases they have significant cost disadvantages' (1965, p. 10). Quantitatively these economies must be significant because of the high levels of transport costs faced by Australian exporters and importers and the high levels of tariff protection on some Australian imports.[3]

Table 4.4 provides the statistics of exports, imports and intra-industry trade for petroleum and petroleum products, Groups 331 and 332 of the SITC, at the 3-, 5- and 7-digit levels in classes accounting for most of the production and trade in refined petroleum products. As in the case of the iron and steel industry, we find that the intra-industry trade percentages are very large even down to the 7-digit level of aggregation in nearly all products except crude petroleum. The explanation of Australia's simultaneous export and import of Aviation kerosene (332.20.02) and Marine diesel fuels (332.30.05) is simply that fuel purchases by foreign carriers in Australia are considered to be exports while those by Australian carriers abroad are considered imports.

The intra-industry trade in the other products is due to a different cause that has not previously been discussed, namely the economics of joint production resulting from the following technical and legal conditions. Since 1964 indigenous crude has been used by Australian refineries, first from the Moonie field in Queensland and later in 1967 from Barrow Island in Western Australia and in 1970 from Gippsland. Until 1970 production and trade were determined essentially by government import policy according to which a price of $3·14 per barrel of indigenous crude was established, based on an 'import parity' formula. This price was substantially in excess of the landed price of imported crudes even when adjustment is made for the superior quality of the light sulphur-free local crudes.[4] To

---

[3] The structure of tariffs within Chapter 73 of the BTN (Iron and steel and articles thereof) is complex. Many steels and steel products outside the range of Australian production enter duty-free. Other duties tend to increase with the degree of fabrication, reflecting the greater relative costs in Australia of products requiring more sophisticated methods and fewer basic materials. Duty collected on all imports of goods classified within Chapter 73 was 13 per cent of the value of these imports in 1968–9 and was between 30 and 40 per cent for several 4-digit tariff items.

[4] Hunter (1969, pp. 11, 26) estimated that the former price for Australian indigenous crude was roughly equivalent to a 43 per cent *ad valorem*

ensure that all Australian crude oil was absorbed in Australian refineries, crude oil of Australian origin was allocated to companies supplying or marketing refined products in proportion to their imports of refinery feedstock and/or refined petroleum products. Heavy contingency duties were levied on imports of these products by importers who failed to take up their allocations of Australian crude.

As a result of these events Australian demand for light refined products, especially motor spirit, in relation to the demand for middle distillate and heavy oils, was greater than the proportions of these oils in total refinery output. Hence additional imports of these products were required at the same time as surplus production of fuel and lubricating oils was exported. This pattern persisted after the refinery companies increased the percentage of light oils produced by means of secondary processing equipment and after some light Australian crude was used by refineries. In sum the petroleum products industry illustrates a case where joint production, with a limited range of products from a plant once installed, which is not matched by complementarity in demand for these products, leads to significant levels of intra-industry trade in functionally homogeneous products.[5]

CHARACTERISTICS OF IMPORTED AND EXPORTED GOODS

Recently Gregory and Tearle (1973) applied the Lancaster goods-characteristics model to refrigerators sold in Australia and estimated the different quantities of characteristics embodied in these refrigerators.[6] Three characteristics or attributes of refrigerators are considered – cubic capacity, and binary

---

tariff, or $US 1·00 per barrel in 1965, rising to 57 per cent in 1968 because of greater discounts from posted f.o.b. prices for foreign crude.

[5] Additional secondary intra-industry trade arises because the northern ports import all their petroleum product supplies to avoid the transport costs around the long Australian coastline.

[6] Kravis and Lipsey (1971) estimate the implicit prices of several groups of commodities exported by industrial countries. These estimates confirm the usefulness of the goods-characteristics model but are less relevant to us than a comparison of the characteristics of goods exported and imported by the same country.

variables indicating whether or not the refrigerator has one or two doors and is frost-free. Regression equations are used to estimate the implicit prices of these characteristics for imported and Australian-produced refrigerators separately and for different years. These equations indicate that there are roughly uniform implicit prices for each attribute in the market, that is, the quantities of goods characteristics do determine consumer purchases. Imported refrigerators combine these characteristics in different quantities from refrigerators produced in Australia. They are smaller, mainly less than 6 ft in cubic capacity, and are simpler, all imports until 1969 having only one door and not being frost-free. Many of them are smaller-model types used in motel and hotel rooms. In contrast, in 1971 over 90 per cent of domestically produced models exceeded 7 cu ft in capacity, 80 per cent exceeded 10 cu ft, and it appears that almost all large refrigerators sold were made in Australia. This pattern of sales is consistent with the estimates of implicit prices for characteristics which predict that imported refrigerators should be cheaper than domestically produced refrigerators only up to 6 cu ft in capacity.

These different goods characteristics for imported and domestically produced goods explain the intra-industry trade in the case of complete refrigerators for which the trade statistics are shown in the first row of Table 4.5. The intra-industry per-

TABLE 4.5
Trade in Refrigerators and Freezers, 1968–9

SITC Item	Description	Exports ($'000)	Imports ($'000)	Intra-Industry Trade* ($'000)	Intra-Industry Trade (%)
	Complete domestic† refrigerators and freezers	597	5885	1194	18
	Parts: total	2025	238	476	21
	Compressors and parts	1805	8	17	0
	Other parts	220	230	440	97
275.01	Total: Domestic refrigerators and freezers, complete and parts	2622	6125	5245	60

* This is $(X_i + M_i) - |X_i - M_i|$.
† That is household refrigerators and freezers.

centage of trade in complete refrigerators and freezers is 18 per cent. This is probably biased upwards by the lack of a breakdown of the data into refrigerators and freezers.

Table 4.5, however, shows a cause of high recorded percentage of intra-industry trade for a 5-digit SITC item which differs from those discussed previously. SITC 275.01 contains data on the trade in finished refrigerators and freezers *and* parts. Intra-industry trade is 60 per cent of the trade in this item because of imbalances in the trade in finished goods and in parts. Australia is a net importer of the finished goods but a net exporter of parts, primarily compressors.[7] This shows again the need for careful disaggregation of statistics before they can be used in the measurement of elasticities or tests of comparative advantage because there is a strong presumption that the costs of, and the comparative advantage in the production of compressors and finished refrigerators are subject to significantly different causes.

SUMMARY AND CONCLUSIONS

Both the measures of intra-industry trade at different levels of aggregation and the case studies in this chapter have shown that intra-industry trade in Australia cannot be explained away by disaggregation. Direct evidence that imported and domestically produced goods within industries do embody different characteristics is further convincing evidence that intra-industry trade is economically meaningful and not just the result of aggregation which combines distinct goods in the same item which may not be related in consumption or production. The demonstration that the imported and domestically produced goods embody different characteristics should be followed by an attempt to explain this specialisation in terms of the comparative advantage and disadvantage of Australian producers due to relative factor prices, economies of scale, transport costs or another of the hypotheses we develop in Part II.

[7] The horizontal exchange of exports and imports of complete refrigerators and freezers, and of parts for each other is 1194+476 = 1670, or only 31 per cent of the total intra-industry for the 5-digit item. Chapter 6 indicates how certain economies of scale may give rise to this vertical specialisation.

Part II Models Predicting Intra-Industry Trade

5 Intra-Industry Trade in Functionally Homogeneous Products

The traditional Heckscher–Ohlin model of international trade is well known and need not be reproduced here. We only wish to repeat the important point that all the famous theorems such as the factor-price equalisation, Rybczynski and Stolper–Samuelson theorems, and much econometric work and the analysis of the effects of tariffs and other policies on trade,[1] are based on a set of important assumptions. Since this and the following two chapters are intended to show how changes in these assumptions can lead to explanations of intra-industry trade it is useful to list them. The main assumptions of the Heckscher–Ohlin model are:

1 Production functions are identical in all countries.
2 Inputs of capital and labour are homogeneous both within and between countries.
3 Consumers' preferences are given exogeneously.
4 The production functions for all commodities are linearly homogeneous.
5 Commodities produced and traded are homogeneous with respect to all functional characteristics and with respect to location, time of use and packaging.
6 There are no joint products in production or consumption.

The first four of these assumptions are unambiguous. However, the nature of product homogeneity specified under assumption 5 requires some elaboration. The most direct and exact way of introducing product differentiation is, following Lancaster's goods-characteristic model (1966), to regard each commodity as possessing some quantities of each of a number of characteristics. Commodities may be differentiated with respect to any set of characteristics. Two products X_A and X_B manufactured in two countries A and B respectively are considered

[1] See, for example, Corden (1971).

to be 'functionally homogeneous' if the following condition is met: if X_A and X_B are put on a shelf next to each other, consumers are indifferent between them. They therefore sell for the same price at one location and time. If products are not functionally homogeneous they are differentiated in the Chamberlinian sense.

Assumption 5 brings out the fact that even though some goods may be functionally homogeneous in this sense, they may still be differentiated with respect to the timing, location or packaging characteristics. Thus, fresh strawberries produced in the northern and southern hemispheres tend to be functionally homogeneous but differentiated by their location and time of economic usefulness. Similarly, the basic chemical – acetyl-salicylic acid – constituting asprin, is functionally homogeneous whether it is in bulk and unbranded or broken into standard consumer tablets and packaged under an advertised label. Yet differentiation through packaging and brand identification is economically very important. Homogeneity of commodities with respect to location, time and packaging arises from the fundamental assumptions that there are zero costs of (a) transport, (b) storage, (c) selling, (d) information, and (e) government interference.

The method of analysis to be followed is to relax only one, or as few as possible, of the six assumptions at one time and to consider how such a relaxation gives rise to intra-industry trade. In the present chapter we relax only the assumption of functional homogeneity retaining all the other features of the Heckscher–Ohlin model. In the following chapter we relax assumptions 4 and 5 only, providing a theoretical explanation for trade in close-substitute manufactures produced under increasing returns to scale. Chapter 7 contains models capable of explaining the existence of intra-industry trade which are based on dynamic changes in resource endowments or production functions which, under assumptions 1–3, are held constant in the traditional comparative static analysis. These dynamic changes are shown to evolve in market economies because of the existence of non-perfect competition and product differentiation as well as the explicit recognition of human and knowledge capital as factors of production.

Two more minor points relating to exposition need to be

made. First, one could argue that the relaxation of any of the Heckscher–Ohlin model assumptions set out above leads to the generation of a new international trade model deserving a new name.[2] In the present study, we disregard this issue and – mainly for the lack of any suitable alternative names – refer to the Heckscher–Ohlin model with changed assumptions, rather than some new model. Second, we intersperse our abstract models with bits of empirical information. This information is not presented in a rigorous manner and often is not documented. Its main purpose is to illustrate certain theoretical propositions. Perhaps it will lead others to more rigorous empirical testing.

We now discuss how the existence of transport, storage and selling costs can give rise to international trade in functionally homogeneous goods and services.

DIFFERENTIATION BY LOCATION

Transport costs have an important influence on the location of production in two types of commodities. First, there are commodities which have a high cost of transport relative to their basic cost of production, such as sand and bricks. Production typically is located close to the source of raw materials, and sales are limited to customers within a certain area around the place of production. The geographic dimensions of the marketing area are determined by costs of transport and of production at all potential sources of supply. Second, there are commodities which deteriorate physically when transported in a raw or processed state, such as fresh vegetables and raw milk. Location of productive facilities for these goods is determined by the availability of suitable land and the proximity of consumers.

Generally, the geographic dimensions of marketing areas for the two types of commodities are determined by resource availability, transport costs and the spatial distribution of consumers. Fig. 5.1 presents a hypothetical set of marketing areas for a commodity X, say sand, for which transport costs are an important determinant of the source of supplies. Points

---

[2] The Ricardian and H.O. models are usually distinguished on the basis of differences in the assumption about production functions; see Caves (1960, Chapter II).

Figure 5.1
Border Trade

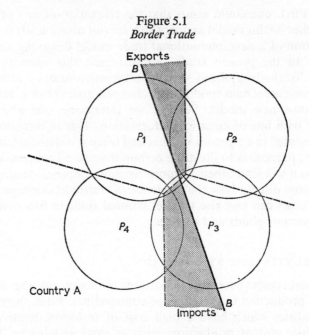

$P_1, \ldots P_4$ indicate the location of four production centres in a given geographic area, and in the absence of any international border. Assume, for simplicity only, that unit costs of production and the transport cost functions are the same at all four production points and that the costs of transport from each production point are proportional to the distance the commodity is transported in any direction. Now draw intersecting circles of *equal* diameter around the four points. Under these conditions production point P_i supplies consumers located in an area bounded by the dotted straight lines drawn between intersections of the four circles. These dotted lines represent loci of points equidistant between centres of two overlapping circles. Every consumer buys from the closest production point in this model.

Now consider the implications resulting from the establishment of two countries, A and B, and the drawing of a national boundary through this territory. In Fig. 5.1 this boundary is represented by the line *BB*. Assuming that the border involves no restrictions on trade and no extra costs to shippers, then

country A, located to the left of the line *BB*, will show in its
international trade statistics exports of commodity *X* equal to
the quantity and value demanded by consumers located in the
area which in Fig. 5.1 is shaded and labelled 'Exports'. The
same country will also show imports of commodity *X*, which
serve residents in the shaded area, labelled 'Imports'. Country *B*
in turn will show analogous intra-industry trade in commodity
X. In the remainder of this book we will refer to this trade in
products which are functionally homogeneous but differentiated
by location as *border trade*.

In the real world the level of border trade depends on all the
factors mentioned in the theoretical analysis, the availability
and cost of producing the commodity, the geographic distribution of consumers and the extent to which national borders
impose transaction costs. These costs consist of direct payments to tariff authorities and of time and resources used up in
filling out customs declarations and exchanging currencies.
Moreover, the uncertainty about future commercial policies in
the foreign country and about the price of foreign exchange
tend to be considered a cost peculiar to sales across the border.
Both the border costs, which can be treated analytically as
transport costs, and the uncertainties of foreign trade modify
the shape of the effective marketing areas, and border trade is a
decreasing function of the height of these barriers.

Geographical characteristics of countries enter into the determination of the level of countries' border trade by determining
costs of production and transport. Rivers, oceans, mountains
and deserts represent natural barriers to trade, often reinforcing
man-made barriers. Generally, we would expect border trade
to be greater, other things being equal, between contiguous
territories. Furthermore, border trade may be related to the
size of the bordering countries. Alfred Marshall noted that 'a
small country has a larger frontier in proportion to her area
than a large country of the same shape'.[3] This proposition may
be expressed formally by the geometry of size (as measured by
a country's area). 'Areas of similar figures necessarily stand to
one another in the proportion of the squares of their several

[3] Marshall (1919, p. 25). Marshall used his geometric propositions to
explain why *per capita* trade is likely to be greater in small than in large
nations.

linear dimensions.'[4] For example, a circle whose area is one-quarter the area of another circle has a circumference only one-half that of the larger circle. A second geometric property of small area is that average distance from the border is less. Again, if one of two circles is four times as large as the other, the average distance from the circumference (border) of the smaller circle is only one-half that of the larger area. One would expect more border trade among small neighbouring countries.

International trade data provide examples of the predictions of the simple model just presented. SITC Class 273, Sand, stone and gravel, probably is the most typical border-trade good that can be found. Its products have high transport costs and are found naturally and mined in many places. Tariffs and other trade restrictions tend to be low. Therefore, it is interesting to note two pieces of information.

First, as can be seen from Table 3.1, border trade in SITC 273 between Canada and the US in 1967–8 showed a *B* value of 96 for both countries, indicating virtual equality of exports and imports. This is as the theory suggests. The common political border between the two countries for the most part is not re-inforced by natural barriers and tends to leave population and land with nearly equal characteristics on both sides.

Second, if one considers the matrix of bilateral trade flows in SITC 273 for the ten OECD countries, the countries in the rows and columns of the matrix can be ordered in such a way that countries with common borders are adjacent to each other. The resultant pattern of the matrix elements suggests strongly that nearly all trade in this commodity occurs among countries having contiguous borders. In Chapter 11 we discuss the technique, difficulties and limitations of matrix analysis for the classification of commodities into different categories of intra-industry trade, including border trade.

We have not been able to produce empirical estimates of intra-industry trade in goods differentiated by location, nor by entering statistics as border trade. However, casual inspection of trade classes and statistics shows that border trade may well be limited to such groups as sand, stone and gravel, fresh fruit, vegetables and dairy products. These considerations imply that

[4] Ibid., p. 25, n. 1.

border trade is not an important ingredient of overall world trade and welfare. Of course, for some regions along borders and some small countries, these forms of trade may be significant. It might be interesting to attempt quantification of border trade by the case study of some regions in North America or Europe.

DIFFERENTIATION BY TIME

There are some goods with limited economic life for which timing of consumption represents an important element of differentiation, even though the commodities otherwise are functionally homogeneous. Examples of goods in this category are seasonal agricultural products and electricity.

Intra-industry trade in these goods is basically due to the fact that their potential or actual domestic prices vary over time because of differences in either supply or demand conditions. Thus, production of fruit in winter in countries with temperate climates is not profitable at prevailing world prices and there are imports from countries with more suitable climate. These same countries, on the other hand, tend to export the same fruits during the summer months. In the case of electricity production, costs are constant through time but demand peaks at certain predictable periods of the day. As a result efficient shadow prices of electricity are different throughout the day. Differences in these shadow prices between two countries at a given moment which are not reflected in prices charged to domestic consumers give rise to intra-industry trade in electricity.

Formally, intra-industry trade in these goods can be fitted into the traditional Heckscher–Ohlin model by assuming that the production-possibility frontier has a different shape in each season or that the indifference maps shift at various times of the day. For example, consider Figs. 5.2a and 5.2b, assumed to represent country A in winter and summer respectively. Product X is the perishable agricultural product and Y is a manufactured product. Other commodities may be produced but it is assumed that the total resources available for the production of X and Y are unchanged over the summer and winter. This is a reasonable approximation since the prices of all other commodities are considered fixed. This enables us to derive the

Figure 5.2
Periodic Goods

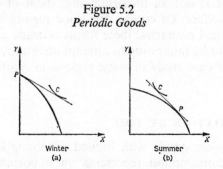

Winter   Summer
(a)   (b)

production-possibility frontier for these two commodities alone.[5] In winter the opportunity frontier shows that product X can be produced only at a great sacrifice in terms of product Y, but in summer the trade-off is more favourable. At the given world prices of X and Y in winter, X is not produced and all domestic consumption of this good is imported. In summer, on the other hand, product X is produced and exported. Consequently, country A's annual statistics of trade show intra-industry trade in both X and Y.

To represent the case of electricity consider Figs. 5.3a and 5.3b which are assumed to represent conditions during the day and evening respectively. The production-possibility frontier for X and Y alone and relative prices are unchanged, yet the public demands electricity (product X) and product Y in different proportions in the evening (OC' in 5.3b) than during the day (OC in 5.3a). Consequently during the day, electricity is exported and in the evening it is imported.

For expositional convenience we will refer to trade in agricultural products, electricity and similar goods as *periodic trade*. This trade is based on predictable, periodic fluctuations in nations' production of or demand for these commodities. Resultant relative market prices of these commodities, costs of producing them and the costs of storage and transport encourage their appearance as simultaneous exports and imports in records of trade spanning more than one period. The tradi-

[5] A similar device has been used in the analysis of the production of public goods; see, for example, Little (1951). This device allows changes in the production and consumption of other individual commodities in response to changes in the prices of X and Y.

Figure 5.3
Electricity

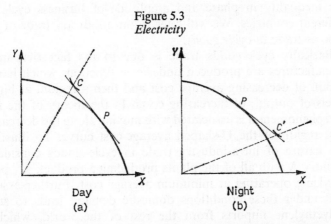

Day
(a)

Night
(b)

tional Heckscher–Ohlin model does not predict the existence of periodic trade goods because either costs of storage and transport are assumed to be zero or the period of analysis is chosen to eliminate reversal of the periodic influences mentioned above.

In the real world countries, periodic intra-industry trade tends to be a decreasing function of countries' geographical size and diversity of climate. The large nations like the US, the Soviet Union and Australia probably have small periodic trade because, for example, national power grids can be used to even out peak local demands in electricity of widely dispersed population and production centres. Similarly the wide range of climatic zones within the same country obviates the need for cyclical goods trade in perishable agricultural products. Conversely the smaller countries of Western Europe probably have relatively larger trade in these products. Generally, however, the absolute level of trade in these commodities is small. It can be expected to grow as electrical power demand rises generally and as lower costs of air transport encourage the shipment of perishable seasonal agricultural products between the northern and southern parts of the world and of continents.

We now turn to the explanation of intra-industry trade in functionally homogeneous goods where timing of sale and storage costs continue to be the determinants of trade but where the pattern is random or cyclical in contrast with the periodic pattern discussed in the preceding section. Intra-industry trade in this category is due to the lumpiness of some investments and the inequality in phase and amplitude of business cycles in different countries. We will refer to intra-industry trade of this type as trade in *cycle goods*.

Basically cycle-goods trade is due to the fact that many manufactures are produced under cost functions which have a region of decreasing average cost and then a region, at higher levels of output, of increasing costs. In the theory of the firm this phenomenon is associated with moving along the decreasing cost region of the U-shaped average-cost curve. To illustrate the nature of intra-industry trade in cycle goods consider a country A with all of the plants producing a product, say polyethylene, operating at minimum average cost. Further assume that under these conditions domestic demand leads to some polyethylene imports from the rest of the world, which is assumed to be unable to consume its own minimum-rate cost output of polyethylene. If within an accounting period for the reporting of international trade statistics, demand for this commodity decreases in country A and increases in country B, then country A will export polyethylene. The statistics for the full period will show intra-industry trade. Elaborate models would be required to produce truly rigorous explanations of cycle-goods trade for inter-country differences in the phasing and amplitudes of business cycles. However, we feel that the case is intuitively obvious enough and does not warrant more detailed analysis.

The lumpiness of many modern investment projects tends to give rise to random patterns of intra-industry trade which may in practice be difficult to distinguish from those caused by business cycles. Many modern industrial plants and mining facilities have long planning and construction periods, their optimum output represents substantial fractions of total domestic or even world demand because of economies of scale in plant size and they have steeply falling average-cost curves up to capacity levels. These conditions are especially pronounced in the chemical, petroleum and copper, and aluminium industries where recently erected polyethylene, fertiliser and gas liquidification plants and alumina and copper mines and smelters are of enormous size. When plants or mines of this kind go into operation they can easily change a country from importer to exporter of these goods. If such a switch in trade patterns occurs during an accounting period, statistics will show the existence of intra-industry trade in functionally homogeneous goods.

We have no empirical evidence in the magnitude of cycle-goods trade. However, we are prepared to speculate that this type of intra-industry trade does not represent a significant fraction of total intra-industry trade.

OTHER INTRA-INDUSTRY TRADE

Another group of functionally homogeneous commodities which give rise to intra-industry trade involves the import and export of goods after storage and wholesaling, known as entrepot trade, and of goods subjected to 'blending, packaging, bottling, cleaning, sorting, husking and shelling . . . which leave them essentially unchanged',[6] known as re-export trade. The traditional Heckscher–Ohlin model can be used to explain why certain countries, such as Hong Kong and Singapore, have a comparative advantage in the provision of services connected with entrepot and re-export trade. Both these cities lie along major sea-routes, are near great populated areas, have natural harbour facilities and have an abundant supply of labour required for the provision of these services.

The goods processed in entrepot and re-export trade are not transformed sufficiently to warrant statistical reclassification between importation and exportation. Thus intra-industry trade is observed. It might be noted though, that many countries present separate statistics on 'normal' trade and entrepot and re-export trade. In general, however, these two special trade categories are relatively small and collections of international trade statistics by supranational organisations such as the OECD or IMF present only consolidated overall trade data.

There is also substantial two-way trade in financial, insurance, shipping, brokerage and related services which are purchased by the exporters or importers of goods. Two of the prime determinants of the demand for and supply of these services are information about the creditworthiness of borrowers and the reliability of brokers, insurers and insured. The cost of obtaining

[6] Australian Commonwealth Bureau of Census and Statistics (1969, p. 4).

information about transactors on these matters is high initially but low at the margin and tends to depreciate rapidly. Local firms doing regular business with exporters and importers, often in connection with domestic business, have accumulated and maintained a stock of relevant knowledge, the additional use of which involves extremely low marginal private and social cost. For these reasons local firms in these services industries tend to enjoy a comparative advantage in supplying their exporters or importers with these services. Since these principles of the economics of information are valid in all countries, statistics tend frequently to show intra-industry trade in services.

It is the existence of positive information costs associated with finance, insurance and related services which leads to intra-industry trade in functionally homogeneous products. Empirically intra-industry trade in these goods probably represents a very small fraction of the total trade of most countries with some exceptions such as Hong Kong and Singapore.

HOMOGENEOUS COMMODITIES AND GOVERNMENT REGULATIONS

When governments intervene in the allocation of resources and international trade it is not difficult to find phenomena which are inconsistent with economic theories. We need not develop any elaborate analysis to prove this point, though it may be useful to distinguish intra-industry trade in homogeneous commodities induced by two types of government actions and regulations.

First, there is the group of government actions which purposely involve the import and export of goods in order to achieve some special social objective. For example, a government might find it socially desirable to subsidise the export of a given product from one region in order to alleviate local unemployment or help an infant industry while another region of the same country imports the same product from abroad. Trade within the country may be prevented by rivalries among regional governments or by the existence of trade agreements among national governments. Nations of the Eastern bloc are known to have entered into numerous trade agreements with Western countries which involve the import of some products for which domestic demand is inadequate or for which re-export at higher prices is profitable, sometimes within the framework of another trade agreement.

A second group of government actions leads unintentionally to the import and export of homogeneous commodities. Many countries have such complicated, interdependent regulations governing economic activity that it is impossible to know precisely the net effect of the entire structure. For example, it has been alleged that tariffs, subsidies and currency control regulations at one point made it profitable for Indian firms to import, unload, reload and export the identical commodity on the identical ship.[7] Undoubtedly some of the trade agreements between centrally controlled Communist countries and Western nations, developed and developing, have resulted in unintended intra-industry trade, though it may be difficult to document such cases and distinguish them from those which were designed to serve some other economic, political or military motive.

The enumeration of intra-industry trade caused by government actions was undertaken more for the sake of analytical completeness than for its likely empirical importance. Policies leading unintentionally to intra-industry trade can be expected to be adjusted promptly as soon as the consequences are apparent. Intra-industry trade by design in homogeneous commodities is almost certain to be an inferior instrument to achieve some social objective. For these reasons this kind of intra-industry trade is likely to be small.

CONCLUSIONS

In this chapter, we have shown that intra-industry trade in functionally homogeneous products can be explained by using the Heckscher–Ohlin model but relaxing its assumptions that costs of transport, storage, selling and information are zero. We believe that the analytical results are interesting and useful in the explanation of a wide range of real world phenomena, border trade in periodic and cyclical goods, and trade induced by governments.

[7] For a careful analysis of Indian experience with a complicated set of regulations, see Bhagwati and Desai (1970).

Unfortunately we have not been able to quantify the magnitude of intra-industry trade in functionally homogeneous products. However, our intuitive judgement suggests that intra-industry trade in functionally homogeneous products is quantitatively not very significant. Moreover its importance is likely to be overshadowed by trade in functionally differentiated products which are close substitutes in production, consumption or both, and which we discuss in the next chapter.

It is worth noting that the preceding models and the analysis of the next two chapters are focused on the explanation of trade patterns[8] but that underlying them are particular sets of production and demand patterns. While we do not dwell on the characteristics of production and demand which give rise to intra-industry trade, for many important policy issues such as economic development, protection and capital flows these domestic factors are as important as the trade implications. In Chapter 11 we return to this point.

[8] Gruber and Vernon (NBER, 1970, pp. 238–48) demonstrate the similarity of exports of manufactures among the principal manufacturing countries. This is also predicted by the models.

6 Differentiated Products and Economies of Scale

Following the approach outlined at the beginning of Chapter 5, we now return to the traditional Heckscher–Ohlin assumption that costs of transport, storage, selling and information are zero. However, we shall relax assumptions 4 and 5 outlined earlier. That is, we now recognise explicitly the existence of economies of scale and of international trade in commodities which are functionally differentiated. In the first part of this chapter, we show that some intra-industry trade in functionally differentiated goods can readily be explained even if there are no economies of scale. Later we consider the implications of the existence of economies of scale for the pattern of international trade in close-substitute products.

PRODUCTS WITH DIFFERENT INPUT REQUIREMENTS

Inspection of the SITC scheme shows that the commodities grouped in aggregates at, say, the 3-digit level may be close substitutes in production, consumption or both. For example, in the class of Inorganic chemicals (SITC 512), large numbers of chemical compounds are aggregated, all of which are produced by rather similar processes and very often by the same firm in the same plants. Yet there is little substitutability in their use. Sulphuric and phosphoric acid in most uses cannot be substituted for each other. Products, such as inorganic chemicals, thus are grouped together because of the similarity of the production processes, input requirements, or both. Other commodity groupings, such as Furniture (821), Jewellery (897) and Textile yarn and thread tend to be characterised by close substitutability in consumption and may or may not require similar production processes or inputs. Thus, there may be furniture made of wood, steel, aluminium and plastic. There may be yarn of acetate, nylon or wool.

As one considers all pairs of 4- (or 5-) digit commodities within each 3-digit SITC item they can be arranged in a two-dimensional array of the kind shown in Fig. 6.1. Along the

Figure 6.1
Groups of Differentiated Products

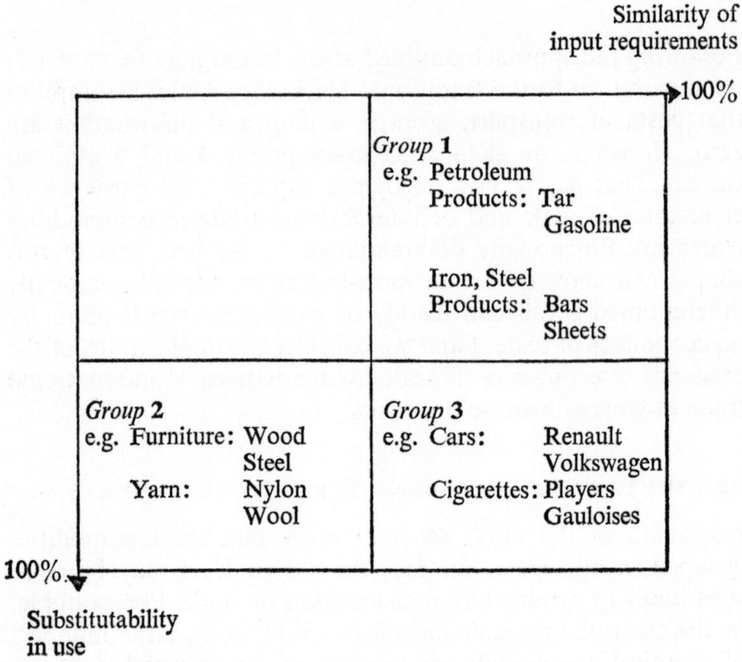

Similarity of
input requirements

▶100%

	Group 1 e.g. Petroleum Products: Tar Gasoline Iron, Steel Products: Bars Sheets
Group 2 e.g. Furniture: Wood Steel Yarn: Nylon Wool	Group 3 e.g. Cars: Renault Volkswagen Cigarettes: Players Gauloises

100%.▼

Substitutability
in use

horizontal axis, we observe the commodity pair's similarity of input requirements, ranging from an index of zero to one hundred, that is, substitutability in production. On the vertical axis is an analogous index of substitutability in consumption or use.

The upper right quadrant (group 1) contains commodities with rather similar input requirements but low substitutability in use, such as petroleum products, gasoline and tar, and iron products, bars and sheets. In the lower left quadrant (group 2) are commodities with high degrees of substitution in use, such as wood and steel furniture and nylon and wool yarn. The lower right quadrant (group 3) shows cars and cigarettes which have similar input requirements and high substitutability in their respective uses. To dramatise the character of this last set of pairs of goods we used dominant brand names from different countries. The upper left quadrant contains no entries since products which are low on the scale of both similarity of input requirements and substitutability in use will not be found in the same industry class. In practice the assignment of a pair of commodities to one of the four groups will be arbitrary.

Intra-industry trade in products of group 2 can readily be explained with the traditional Heckscher–Ohlin model assuming constant return to scale in production.[1] Input requirements for the production of different types of furniture (wood and steel) and yarn (nylon and wool) are so different that the principle of comparative advantage can be applied in its simplest form to explain why countries can be found importing and exporting simultaneously two products within the same group. For this group of goods the intra-industry trade phenomenon is simply the result of statistical aggregation. Analytically, therefore, it is the least interesting of the three groups. Quantitatively, we would venture the guess that it may be reasonably important. The development of synthetic substitute materials and of modern material-processing facilities has led to the availability of wide varieties of substitute products made from different materials. For example, retail stores in many countries carry furniture not only of wood and steel, but also of wicker, bamboo and plastic materials, manufactured by processes with different degrees of labour-intensity.

Group 1 goods can usefully be separated into two different subsets. The first of these consists of products which are distinct but which, as a result of technical peculiarities, tend to be manufactured in fixed proportions or proportions which can be altered only at high costs. The outstanding examples of such goods are petroleum derivatives such as tar, gasoline and oils of different weights. It is easy to envisage that countries may have domestic demand patterns which, at existing world prices, result in excess demand or excess supply of different petroleum derivatives. Our case study of Australia's trade in petroleum products presented in Chapter 4 illustrates this proposition.

[1] The variants considered in the previous chapter also appear here.

Analytically it is the joint-product technology combined with international differences in demand (or in derived demand for inputs) which give rise to the intra-industry trade in this class of goods. All assumptions of the traditional Heckscher–Ohlin model, except the one ruling out joint products, can be fulfilled and yet intra-industry trade exists. Empirically, trade in joint products of this type is limited in many industries because processes changing the properties of certain joint products are available. For example, in the petroleum industry, cracking and polymerisation can be used to produce almost any desired properties of heavy and light fuels. However, once in existence, these cracking and polymerisation plants cannot readily be adjusted to produce different output mixes.

The second subset of commodities in group 1 consists of commodities such as iron and steel products (i.e. bars, rods, beams, sheets, wires, each of different dimensions and quality) which are made from similar materials and frequently in the same plant and machine. These are now considered, first without economies of scale and then with such economies.

PRODUCTS WITH SIMILAR INPUT REQUIREMENTS AND ECONOMIES OF SCALE

Consider the standard Heckscher–Ohlin model with all of the assumptions specified in Chapter 5. There may be any number of products but we shall consider only two among them. Since the production functions for both products are assumed to be linearly homogeneous, for any given relative input prices the input proportions are constant for all outputs. Identical input requirements mean, therefore, that the two products use identical input proportions for all levels of output of the two products. Assuming the supply of primary inputs is fixed, the transformation surface in multiproduct space will have the special property that the marginal rate of transformation between the two products with identical input proportions is constant everywhere on the surface.[2]

Now we introduce the fact that, in certain industries, de-

[2] For the constancy of the marginal rate of transformation when there are only two products with identical input proportions see Kemp (1969, p. 26). The property can be generalised immediately to many products.

veloped countries tend to produce large numbers of substitute products with input requirements within each country so similar that they may be considered identical. Thus France produces not only Gauloises cigarettes but many other brands. In Britain one finds the manufacture of Players along with many other brands. Analogous conditions prevail in the car industry and a large number of other industries. The Heckscher–Ohlin model also assumes the identity of production functions across countries. These input proportions are presumably fixed for technological reasons, and these reasons are assumed to apply to all countries. Therefore the constant rates of transformation between these products and their relative prices must be the same across countries. As a result the exchange of these commodities with identical input requirements for each other is not profitable, because profits arise from the exploitation of differences in relative prices among countries. Yet we observe the exchange of such products. The inconsistency between the theory and reality can be explained by relaxing either the assumption that the production functions are identical across countries or the assumption that there are no economies of scale. We shall now relax the latter assumption. Differences in technology across countries are considered in the next chapter.

Increasing returns have been considered in the literature on the pure theory of international trade. However, as we have already noted at the beginning of this chapter, it has usually been assumed that the economies of scale are a function of plant size and that products are produced in different plants. In this analysis we depart from the traditional analysis and assume that the products are close but imperfect substitutes in consumption, have identical input requirements and are produced in the same plant. The economies of scale are a function of the length of production runs of each product.[3] In Chapter 1 we discussed the nature of these economies of scale and reviewed some evidence of them. It will be recalled that the cost savings are due primarily to the reduced downtime of machines, greater specialisation of machines and labour and to smaller inventories of inputs and output.

Assuming the production of other products is held constant,

[3] The length of production runs as a determinant of trade has been considered by Verdoorn (1960), Drèze (1960) and Daly *et al.* (1968).

we may derive the production-possibility frontier for two such representative differentiated products. Unlike the production-possibility frontier with constant returns to scale for all products, this frontier may have sections which are concave from above and it may be strictly concave from above, as in Fig. 6.2.[4]

Figure 6.2
Trade with Economies of Scale

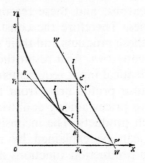

In this version of the model, the relative price of the two commodities depending on the particular point of production P is the point of production under autarky, resulting in the relative price RR.

Now consider the consequences of trade in X and Y at the world price ratio WW shown in Fig. 6.2. Country A can now specialise in the production of either good X or Y.[5] In the graph we have assumed that production will be at P', consumption at C' and welfare given by the community indifference level $I'I'$. The most important conclusion from this analysis is that trade is profitable even if products have identical input requirements.[6]

[4] So far as the shape of the production frontier is concerned this case is analogous to that of single-product production functions with increasing returns to scale; see Herberg and Kemp (1969).

[5] The important question of whether producers responding to market prices will go to the point at which social welfare is maximised is discussed in Chapter 8.

[6] This concept is somewhat ambiguous under conditions of increasing returns. With economies of scale, inputs per unit of output will decrease for either product as that product is increased. More precisely, therefore,

This increasing returns to scale modification of the Heckscher-Ohlin model yields another competing explanation of intra-industry trade. There is nothing inherent in the pattern of intra-industry trade which allows us to rank the explanations in terms of their empirical importance. We believe that the explanation based on economies of scale just presented is quantitatively the most important for the following reasons. First, there are industries in which the production conditions are consistent with the above assumptions. There are large numbers of industries with high volume and value of trade which are characterised by products differentiated in minor ways relevant to the consumers' satisfaction. This differentiation requires negligible adjustments to the basic production process on the one hand but leads to costly machine downtime, inventories, selling costs, etc. on the other. A selected list of industries in this category contains processed foods, beverages (alcoholic and non-alcoholic), textiles, clothing, shoes, cars, motor-cycles, bicycles, furniture, tobacco products, appliances, hand-tools, aeroplanes, boats; producers goods such as presses, drills, lathes, cutting tools, electronic and mechanical data-processing equipment, communications equipment and chemical-processing plants. There exist independent theoretical and some empirical evidence on the importance of economies of scale resulting from the increased length of runs and scale (see Chapter 1).

Second, countries trading in these products have similar endowments with human, knowledge and real capital relative to labour and land, to make it highly unlikely that the minor differences in input requirements between goods within each of these industries could lead to the large observed trade if production were subject to constant returns to scale.

Third, the dynamics of adjustment following economic integration, the general growth of economies and reduction in transport costs in the presence of economies of scale are also consistent with observed facts. We now outline some aspects of dynamic adjustment to changes in trading conditions.

---

the conditions of identical input requirements is defined as identical input requirements per unit of output in the products concerned at each level of output. This implies that the transformation surface in Fig. 6.2 is symmetric about the ray from the origin at an angle of 45°.

THE PATTERN OF SPECIALISATION WITH ECONOMIES OF SCALE

In our model with no trade in products X and Y, country A produced both differentiated goods as at the point P in Fig. 6.2. At this point the domestic price ratio (P_x/P_y) is equal to the tangent RR. Now assume that, in the rest of the world, there exist products X' and Y' which are close substitutes to country A's products X and Y in the sense that consumers are indifferent between the two corresponding competing brands or styles of X and X' (and similarly Y and Y') when offered at identical prices. Production functions in the rest of the world and country A are identical but because of assumed differences in preferences and production price ratios are $(P_x/P_y) < (P_x'/P_y')$.

Now consider the consequences of removing the barriers to trade between country A and the rest of the world for goods X and Y only. At existing relative prices between X and Y, country A's good X is relatively cheaper than its close substitute X' while Y is more expensive than Y'. Competition in country A may lead to increased production of X and decreased production of Y until complete specialisation is reached as in Fig. 6.2. However, this is by no means the only possible outcome. In a model with international trade in differentiated products, the result of freeing trade will depend, in general, on the initial production of the trading countries, the reaction of producers to increased competition, the rates of gross investment by producers in all countries, the general patterns of comparative advantage. It would be a tedious exercise to consider all the possibilities but we can make some general points.

One possibility is that at the equilibrium exchange rate following the removal of trade barriers certain industries in country A may retain production in all of their differentiated product lines or lose all of them simply because economies of scale are sufficiently small to impart comparative advantage or disadvantage of the traditional kind for the industry as a whole despite the economies of scale.

Another aspect is that the production and marketing of the kinds of commodities considered in this analysis typically is dominated by oligopolistic market structures in which advertising and collusive behaviour of all sorts play an important role in the determination of competitive behaviour. The model we have presented could be enriched and made more realistic by the explicit recognition of the oligopolistic market structure in the analysis of the dynamic adjustment process. We have not done so, partly because the general tendencies are intuitively easy to see and partly because these kinds of models are often indeterminate or based on particular assumptions, the validity of which is questionable.[7]

The hypothetical opening of trade concept has its empirical counterpart in a reduction in transport costs as well as protection. The former represents a gradual process leading to international specialisation in differentiated products of the kind under discussion even in the absence of dramatic tariff reductions and economic integration studied most intensively in the existing literature (see Chapter 1). Economic growth by itself may have the same effects since enlarging domestic markets lowers average costs by increasing the length of runs. Consequently it can become privately and socially profitable to sell abroad. The domestic brand or style in which costs have fallen sufficiently to compete with the closest substitutes in the rest of the world may now be exported, even with constant tariffs and transport costs.

It may be worth closing this section by pointing out some real world developments which are broadly consistent with the conclusions of the simple model we presented. It is well known that, in the EEC, France and Germany started the process of integration, each having a large number of independent automobile producers. Domestic demand conditions, the availability of substitutes to domestically produced cars, the cost of importing and servicing foreign makes, costs of production and marketing, etc. led to a domestic oligopolistic market equilibrium in which profits were maximised. Small producers had found it possible to exist by product differentiation appealing to a sufficiently large proportion of the market. However, as tariff barriers were removed, several types of differentiation from the two countries turned out to be extremely close substitutes for

---

[7] Moreover, there is still no satisfactory analysis using general equilibrium, of international trade with imperfectly competitive markets. This has been lamented by Chipman (1965, p. 737), Johnson (1967, and NBER, 1970, p. 15) and Bhagwati (NBER, 1970, p. 23).

each other. Whichever firm producing one of these closely competing models, sizes or styles had the largest runs, lowest cost, or both, increased its sales and enjoyed still larger cost savings. The competing models experienced reduced sales and increased costs. Many of the small car manufacturers existing in 1958 were unable to adjust their differentiation to meet this foreign competition. Many of them in both France and Germany, such as Borgward, Lloyd, NSU, Simca and Citroën, either went bankrupt or were absorbed by the larger firms and integrated into a European-wide pattern of product differentiation. Europe now enjoys a similar spectrum of styles and sizes as before the integration, perhaps larger, because of overall growth in income and average lower cost of production, but each style and size is produced at lower average cost because of the increased length of runs.

Similar developments have been observed in other consumer-goods industries such as prepared foods, soaps and detergents, sporting goods, clothing and shoes. National brands, once only known to tourists, now appear alongside domestic substitutes on the shelves of retailers in all countries of the EEC. Room has been made on these shelves by the death of some domestic substitutes. The same process of brand, style and quality integration has probably also taken place in producer capital goods and intermediate products, though the results are not as noticeable to the casual observer as they are in consumer goods. Adler (1960) has documented the increased intra-industry specialisation in the iron and steel industries.

The international interpenetration of oligopolistic markets has occurred also between countries which are not part of a customs union or otherwise benefiting from mutual reductions in trade barriers. Japanese cameras have invaded the Western European market while European cameras still sell in Japan. US electronic computers compete domestically and in Japan and Europe with locally produced close substitutes. US watches sell in Switzerland while the United States remains one of the main markets for Swiss watches. The United States iron and steel market has been penetrated by foreign producers while US exports to the same countries continue. Sporting goods of all kinds, razor blades, tobacco products, clothing, patent medicines, branded and advertised, are produced and marketed world-wide by many countries. Often, as we noted in the Introduction, this marketing has been followed by the establishment of local production facilities.

In nearly all instances this international trade seems to be based on relatively minor product differentiation which gives rise to the kinds of economies of scale from length of runs we postulated in our model. The examples given, of course, do not prove the point that these economies of scale are responsible for this world-wide interpenetration of oligopolistic markets and the resultant phenomenon of intra-industry trade. Our arguments merely show that the real world phenomena listed are *consistent with* the postulated model. There are several other, competing hypotheses with which the empirical phenomena are consistent (Chapter 9 pursues this point).

THE NATURE OF PRODUCT DIFFERENTIATION AND TRADE

The preceding section has shown how production and demand conditions lead to a determinate pattern of specialisation of each of our two countries in either of two representative goods X or Y. We purposely neglected the specification of what distinguishes these two products. Now we wish to comment further on the nature of product differentiation and some of the determinants of the products in which a country is likely to specialise. In so doing, we will draw on the work by Linder and Drèze outlined in the Introduction.

Product differentiation may be considered as being of two types, style and quality. In the real world these analytical classes tend to overlap, but basically quality differentiation is based on measurable performance characteristics of products while style differentiation is based on product appearance and marginal performance characteristics, often exaggerated by advertising. Thus, automobiles differing according to size, weight, engine power, durability of finish, etc. are considered to be quality differentiated.

Style Differentiation

With these definitions in mind we return to our basic model and the analysis underlying Fig. 6.2.[8] Consider that X and Y are

[8] The approach to be followed here was first suggested by Corden (1970).

differentiated by style, say light and small Scandinavian furniture (X) and the more traditional, heavier designs (Y). With no trade, country A – say Sweden – would produce both styles to satisfy domestic demand.

In the rest of the world (country B) extremely close substitutes to both styles of furniture are produced and consumed under autarky. Now, in order to get the result that country A ends up specialising in X, and B in Y, we assume that, with no trade, country B consumes a greater proportion of Y relative to X than does country A. Because of the assumed identity of the production functions in both countries under these conditions the price ratio line for X and Y in B is steeper than in A. In Fig. 6.2 the line WW represents such a relative price. Under the usual assumption that A is a small country and B is the rest of the world, the opening of trade does not alter the 'rest of the world' price. At this price, of course, country A will maximise its welfare by specialising in the production of good X.[9]

The preceding analysis yields the important result that the pattern of international trade in close-substitute products differentiated by style takes the form of countries exporting styles most popular with its own population while they import styles appealing to minority tastes. This analytical result leads to a rather straightforward empirically testable hypothesis, which unfortunately we were not able to carry out. However, casual empirical evidence supports this hypothesis. At one time US shirts with buttoned collars were exported throughout the world. US colonial-style furniture is exported in spite of the labour-intensity of its production and high transport costs. Countries tend to export automobile styles which have the largest market shares domestically. Distinctive Japanese (or oriental) shoes, wooden shoes from the Netherlands, stylish lightweight shoes from Italy are exported widely. Prepared food products, such as cheeses, alcoholic beverages, biscuits and chocolates are exported from the countries in which the brands and varieties were developed.

We know of only one study of trade patterns in style differentiated products. This study by Drèze (1960, 1961) developed and tested a hypothesis which is a variant of our more general

[9] We ignore here the possibility that the smaller country may import both products in return for exports of the products of other industries.

model. Drèze argued that small countries, such as his native Belgium, did not have sufficiently large numbers of consumers with homogeneous national tastes to permit the production of styles in runs of a length sufficient to keep costs of production of these styles competitive with available imported substitutes.[10] Therefore, he argued, Belgium will import products differentiated by style from other countries where these styles are domestically most popular. Belgian manufacturers in these industries produce and export styles free from national taste influences, such as white china, used in certain classes of restaurants throughout the world. The Belgian producers presumably at one time had been producing more differentiated styles, but the growth of output and specialisation abroad, lowered transport costs, increased freedom of trade, etc. created competitive pressures resulting in this pattern of style specialisation and output runs of sufficient length to assure survival of these industries. Drèze's empirical study of Belgian trade data broadly confirmed this hypothesis.

Even if it turns out quite generally that international trade in close-substitute products can be explained by style differentiation based on national taste, further interesting questions can be raised about the determination of these national tastes. Is this taste determination related to economic factors or is it entirely in the realm of historic, sociological and political development and thus largely outside the realm of economics? The answer probably is that economic forces played an important role along with these other developments.

There are some case studies of how socio-economic and historical-political factors have entered into the determination of tastes and the pattern of trade.[11] For example, the socialist Swedish Government, in its effort to provide adequate housing for all, produced or encouraged the production of small flats and houses. This small living space in turn encouraged the development of what is now known as Scandinavian furniture, which is small, light, brightly coloured and of the quality of workmanship appropriate for Sweden's high-income levels. By

[10] A similar argument has been made for developing countries producing standardised or 'mature' products by the exponents of the product cycle; see Hirsch (1967).

[11] These studies were suggested to us by H. W. Arndt.

analogy one could argue that the heavy colonial-style furniture of the United States was developed in response to the relative cheapness of land, corresponding sizes of houses, and the special demands of frontier life. In recent decades, as the tendency to live in smaller apartments has spread to other countries and incomes have risen, the Scandinavian furniture has been exported widely. At the same time, however, in many countries there remain some customers with the income, size of home and tastes, which result in US exports of colonial-style furniture.

Historical and political factors may have been more important in the determination of the tastes of the German public for Turkish and of the British public for Virginia blend cigarettes. Britain had encouraged tobacco imports from its American colonies while Germany had a traditional political and military tie with Turkey. Similarly the historic British relationship with India helped the development of a public preference for tea while most of the other European countries consume proportionately more coffee than tea.

The preceding kind of analysis is characterised by *ad hoc* explanations tailored to individual cases. The evidence is difficult to refute because it involves many judgements about historic trends, the meaning and implications of alliances and government policies for which objective information may not be obtainable. For this reason the preceding analysis of the determination of taste and patterns of trade in style-differentiated products may be disliked by theorists trained in the tradition of formulating rigorous tests of simple hypotheses. In all likelihood the two approaches will complement each other and increase our understanding of the pattern of world trade.

Differentiation by Quality

The basic approach used in the development of our model for the prediction of trade patterns in style-differentiated products can readily be used for the case where product differentiation is based on quality differences. As an illustration, we make the following assumptions. First, one product Y is of higher quality than another product X. Second, consumers in country A choose between X and Y on the basis of their incomes. Thus, for example, persons with incomes above $5000 per year consume Y, those below $5000 consume X. Third, the income distributions in countries A and B (the rest of the world) overlap as, for example, in Fig. 6.3.

Figure 6.3
Income and Quality of Products Demanded

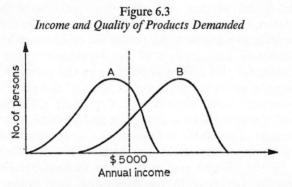

From this set of assumptions it follows that country A will produce and consume proportionately more of the lower-quality product X than of Y because the majority of its population has an income of less than $5000 per year. If the countries differ greatly in the size of total population this factor should be included as a determinant of total domestic demand. This consumption proportion is assumed to be indicated by the slope of the ray from the origin through the point P in Fig. 6.2. After this step the analysis is identical to that developed in the case of product differentiation by style. Relative demand in B is such that the world price WW is established after the opening of trade. The pre-trade relative price in A is assumed to lead to specialisation in X. In the new equilibrium, trade essentially amounts to country A supplying the poorer-income units of country B with the lower-quality good while the richer segments of the population in A are supplied by imports of Y from country B.

This model represents an adaptation of the basic idea first developed by Linder and outlined in the Introduction. It produces the prediction that the pattern of intra-industry trade in quality-differentiated goods, requiring nearly identical inputs and being subject to increasing returns to scale, is determined by the relationship between countries' income distributions and the elasticity of demand for quality with respect to levels of income. This result leads to the most simple, empirically verifiable hypothesis that a high-average-income country should export relatively high-quality and import relatively low-quality products.

Linder found evidence supporting this hypothesis in the trade of his native Sweden. To the best of our knowledge it has not been possible to replicate these results for other countries or for more elaborate formulations of the hypothesis.[12] One of the main causes for this failure appears to be the inability to find unambiguous empirical measures of 'quality' differences which hold constant other dimensions of product differentiation. However, the hypothesis is appealing and probably correct for a wide range of products and countries with income differences above a minimum threshold. Furthermore it seems to be supported by the historic evolution of the trade pattern of such countries as Germany in the nineteenth and Japan in the twentieth centuries. In the last half of the nineteenth century when Germany was attempting to industrialise and catch up with Britain, cheap and low-quality German manufactures were exported. Japan similarly went through a period where its manufactures were known for low quality and price. It need hardly be documented that these two countries experienced a simultaneous increase in their domestic *per capita* incomes, in domestic demand for and production of high-quality goods and the export of these goods for lower-quality imports from other countries.

Trade in Differentiated Capital Goods

Quality and style differentiation in consumer goods have their analogue in intermediate raw materials such as steel in various shapes and qualities, and fixed capital goods such as lathes and presses. In these categories of goods domestic conditions of demand and factor prices also tend to determine the pattern of intra-industry specialisation. For example, high-income, urbanised countries using much steel in construction of tall buildings and bridges will tend to specialise in the production and export of shapes and qualities of steel required for this purpose.

[12] Grubel (1967) reports abortive attempts to test these hypotheses more generally. Hufbauer (NBER, 1970, pp. 197–206) does a test of the Linder hypothesis but, as noted by Keesing (NBER, pp. 277–8), the test should have used data of bilateral trade rather than global trade flows.

Similarly, automated lathes are in greater demand in countries with high capital–labour ratios and production of this type is concentrated there.[13]

Economies of scale due to the length of production run (and those due to the size of plant) indicate the possibility that the specialisation across countries may take the form of what may be called vertical intra-industry specialisation in contrast to the horizontal intra-industry specialisation in different final products. The models in this chapter, and in other sources quoted, are presented as if the commodities concerned are final commodities and they concern horizontal specialisation. Vertical intra-industry specialisation may take several forms. It may involve the exchange between countries of certain final products by an industry for intermediate products used by the industry.[14] Chapter 4 cites an example in Australia in which the Australian refrigerator industry exports compressors and other refrigerator parts and imports complete refrigerators. Another possibility is that two countries may exchange different parts, components or raw materials used in the production of commodities by the industry. They may or may not at the same time also exchange different final products of the industry.

In all these cases of vertical intra-industry trade the statistics group the raw materials, intermediate and final products in one category. However, international trade statistics do not classify goods according to whether they are used as intermediate or final goods and it is not, therefore, possible in general to distinguish between vertical and horizontal intra-industry specialisation.

To conclude this chapter, we note that our theoretical intra-industry trade models rely on the definition of 'industries' which is theoretically precise and corresponds to the definition used in price and industrial organisation theory. The difficulties with the concept of an industry discussed in Chapter 1 are due solely to practical application of the theoretical concept to the analysis of actual trade flows.

---

[13] Kravis and Lipsey (1971, especially pp. 57–8) give other examples of capital goods developed for local markets and exported.

[14] The international exchange of final products or raw materials on the one hand, for fixed capital equipment on the other, is more likely to be inter-industry specialisation since the fixed capital goods are more commonly manufactured in machinery and specialised industries.

7 Intra-Industry Trade through Technology, Product Cycles and Foreign Processing

The first two parts of the present chapter are based on the literature concerned with international trade in goods in which the producing countries have a temporary comparative advantage due to either legal or natural protection, such as patent and copyright laws and dynamic economies of scale.[1] International trade in these goods is known as 'technological gap' or 'product-cycle' trade. Its nature and causes will be analysed in the first part of this chapter. It will be seen that the arguments presented there are independent of any assumptions about intra-industry trade. The integration of the theories of technological gap and of intra-industry trade is undertaken in the second part of the chapter. This section closes with a general methodological criticism of the technology-gap and product-cycle analysis.

The concluding part of this chapter deals with intra-industry trade arising from the export, foreign processing and reimport of goods, mostly carried out by multinational enterprises taking advantage of lower labour costs abroad. These manufacturing processes often are very labour-intensive and constitute an integral part of the entire production of the products.[2] The activity is known as foreign 'sourcing' or 'processing'. Neither of these terms appears to be perfect, but to simplify exposition we shall refer to the activity as 'foreign processing'. In this form of intra-industry trade for vertically integrated internationally spread industries, the goods traded are goods which are ultimately incorporated in the same final products. Technological-

---

[1] Posner (1961), Hufbauer (1966), Vernon (1966), Hirsch (1967) and papers in the volume published by the NBER (1970).
[2] This part draws heavily on the perceptive article by Helleiner (1973), who in part draws on earlier work by Adam (1971), Leontiades (1971) and Baranson (1971) and who gives several other references to articles in which the phenomenon is discussed.

gap and product-cycle trade goods in contrast are normally considered as distinct and final products, though there is nothing in the theories which restricts this trade to final products.

TECHNOLOGICAL-GAP AND PRODUCT-CYCLE TRADE

Entrepreneurs in capitalist societies have the opportunity to earn extraordinary profits by improving technology and products. Imitation of these improvements by competitors tends to eliminate these profits, giving rise to a process which Schumpeter has called 'the perennial gale of creative destruction'.[3] While this process has been identified as one of the most important forces advancing the overall standard of living in capitalist societies, it has a built-in dilemma. Entrepreneurs will invest in the development of new technology and design of new products only if the expected return through extraordinary profits is sufficiently high and certain, given alternative investment opportunities. The level and certainty of the returns depend on the protection that the innovators enjoy from their competitors' imitations. Thus maximum innovation rates could be obtained by total legal protection of the innovators from their competitors. However, such total legal protection has the disadvantage that all the fruits of the innovations accrue to the innovators and would not be passed on to consumers, as for example through lower product prices in the case of an innovation causing a lower cost of production. The dilemma is that protection of innovators increases the rate of improvement in technology and products but reduces overall benefits to society from them. Capitalist countries have resolved this dilemma through the introduction of patent and copyright laws, which provide innovators protection limited for between five and seven years while assuring unrestricted distribution of the benefits of the innovation thereafter.

Governmental protection of innovators through these laws often merely reinforces the natural protection that commercial secrecy and dynamic economies of scale provide for innovators. In some goods and techniques of production the natural protection assures extraordinary profits for the innovator even

---

[3] Schumpeter (1942).

after his patents or copyrights have expired. In general, however, innovators find it useful to obtain legal protection wherever possible.

The existence of legal and natural protection for innovations in production technology and product design gives rise to technology-gap and product-cycle trade basically because domestic and foreign competitors are unable to obtain information necessary to become rivals to the innovator. As a result, entrepreneurs in the innovating country enjoy a temporary comparative advantage resulting in domestic production and exports, both of which may cease once the protection has ended and the normal laws of comparative advantage assert themselves. In the context of the analytical approach set out in Chapter 5 the assumption of the traditional Heckscher–Ohlin model which is relaxed is the one concerning the identity of production functions in all countries. The protection afforded innovators results in a temporary but effective difference in production functions in countries A and B. However, we note in the last section of this chapter a criticism which obviates the need to relax this particular assumption.

An analytically useful distinction will be drawn between technological-gap and product-cycle trade. For this purpose we define all innovative activity leading to the improvement of production methods as resulting in technology-gap trade. Innovations in styling or performance of products manufactured with basically unchanged technology are considered to result in product-cycle trade. In this last category of trade, product differentiation, advertising and imperfect competition play an important role while they do not necessarily do so in the technology-gap trade. The term 'cycle' refers to the time-path of development, production, export, import and, finally, to ceased production of the new good by the innovating country.

We shall now attempt to give greater precision to the concepts of technology-gap and product-cycle trade by contrasting them first with trade in 'normal' goods analysed in the traditional Heckscher–Ohlin model and, second, with trade under conditions where protection is absent. Our analysis is focused on Fig. 7.1 where the horizontal axes of all three panels measure time. The cost of production, rate of output and rate of trade of goods X and Y in the small country A are shown on the vertical axis of panels I to III respectively. The time-paths shown are considered to be representative of pure analytical cases. But since pure cases rarely occur in the real world, these time-paths are only illustrative and should not be interpreted as the description of necessary cycles.

Technological-Gap Trade

We shall first consider technological-gap trade and assume that good X is undifferentiated and produced in country A at price P_0 and constant quantities OM_0. It is convenient to assume that there is only one producer operating several plants in A under conditions of increasing marginal cost, and that world demand for these products is static, consisting only of replacement demand. All markets are initially in equilibrium.

The dynamic event changing cost, output and trade is assumed to be the invention of a new, cheaper process of production for X at time t_0. The process is patented and becomes available freely to the rest of the world producers at time t_2. The cost of producing X falls between t_0 and reaches its long-run least cost P_1 before t_2, as is shown in panel I by the line P_0XY. The cost falls gradually because of the learning by doing of the workers and managers, getting the 'bugs' out of the new process, placement of new machines, etc.

Good X is assumed to be the 'normal' good. According to panel II, after t_0 the output rises slowly at first as the cost advantage of the new process is small and the process itself is unreliable. Panel III shows reduction of imports. As time progresses the increase in output accelerates and then slows down again until it reaches a maximum of OQ_m at t_4. The shape of the curve is determined by the rate of substitution of the new for the old technique and by the inroads that the cheaper good X makes on domestic and foreign substitutes. For a number of psychological and technical reasons beyond the scope of this analysis, the introduction of new process and goods in the real world appears to follow time-paths resembling the S-curve shown in panel II.[4] At OQ_m, output equals replacement demand in the assumed static world.

Panel III shows that, after t_0, imports of X fall, reaching

[4] Bright (1964) and Rogers (1962) give some technical and psychological reasons in support of the S-shaped time-path.

zero at t_1. After that point, exports grow, following generally the S-curve time-path found for total production, levelling off when foreign replacement demand reaches OE_m. As can be seen, the important time of patent lapse, t_2, has no effect on the output or trade in the normal good X in which country A has attained a comparative advantage and a permanent export position through the assumed improvement in production technology.

Let us now analyse the time-pattern of output and trade in good Y, which we assume to be the technological-gap good. Initially, and during patent protection, output and trade in good Y parallel those of good X, as can be seen from panels II and III. However, after t_2 and the lapse of the patent, the special characteristic of the technological-gap good becomes apparent. At t_2, foreign production starts, exports decline, domestic output increases at a slower rate and reaches an absolute maximum at t_3. At this point, exports cease and imports grow until at t_5 they reach a maximum OM_m. At t_5, output is assumed to have fallen below the level which existed before the technological innovation at t_0. The essential characteristic of good Y therefore is seen to be development of exports (or reduction of imports) during the time of the patent protection between t_0 and t_2 and the subsequent decrease in output and exports. The innovating country A does not have a comparative advantage in the production of Y in the traditional sense in which it has this advantage in the production of X. Higher production, exports and the reduction in the import of Y are due solely to the temporary protection afforded the innovator in production technology.

Product-Cycle Trade

Very few modifications in the preceding analysis need to be made to explain product-cycle trade. Instead of assuming that X and Y are homogeneous products before and after t_0, we consider that, at t_0, product innovation results in goods X' and Y' dominating their respective substitutes X and Y. The prices of the new goods do not necessarily fall, as is shown in panel I. Instead the shake-down period may be considered as involving perfection of the good in its operation or the growing consumer acceptance after an advertising campaign. The main result of

Figure 7.1
Technological-Gap and Product-Cycle Trade

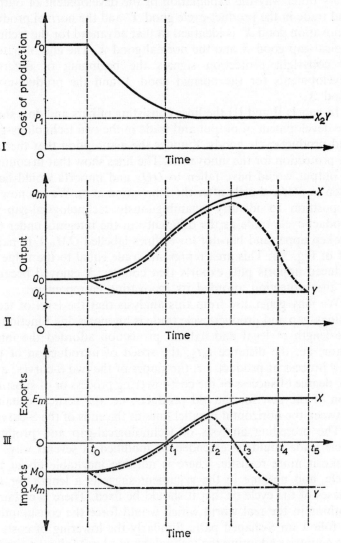

these shake-down or selling periods is the slow growth of domestic output, reduction in imports and growth in exports, which was characteristic of the technological-gap goods. In every other way the explanation of the development of output and trade in the product-cycle good Y' and the normal product innovation good X' is identical to that advanced for the technological-gap good X and the normal good X. The end of patent or copyright protection signals the beginning of different developments for the normal good X and the product-cycle good X.

In panels II and III the lines consisting of bars and dots show the development of output and trade in the two technology-gap and product-cycle goods Y under the assumption that there is no protection for the innovators. The lines show that in country A output would have fallen to OQ_k and imports would have risen to OM_m shortly after the innovation at t_0. We are now in a position to identify unambiguously technological-gap or product-cycle trade as the difference in the integrals under the broken upper and bar-dot lower lines labelled OM_mY in panel III of Fig. 7.1. This area represents trade equal to the value of reduced imports plus exports that country A enjoyed because of the protection afforded its innovating entrepreneur.

We may generalise from this analysis that the level of technology-gap and product-cycle trade is an increasing function of the length of legal and natural protection afforded the innovator, i.e. the distance t_0t_2; the speed of introduction of the new process or product, i.e. the slopes of the two S-curves; and the degree of success of the cost-lowering process or of substitution of the new for the old products, i.e. the vertical distance between the horizontal parallel lines at the ends of the S-curves.

The preceding analysis of technological-gap and product-cycle trade could be extended or modified in several ways to make it more realistic. There is nothing inevitable about the cycle, and nothing in the argument suggests a length for the phases of the cycle or that it should be fixed. There is certainly nothing in the real world which would force the consumption to follow an S-shaped path. Similarly the lowering of costs in the countries adopting the technology need not follow a similar path to that of the innovating country. These former countries may lack the human capital or the complementary overhead capital to take advantage of the innovation and, consequently, their costs may not fall as much or as rapidly as they did in the innovating country. One recent view of innovation which would support this possibility is that put forward by Atkinson and Stiglitz (1969). In their view some innovations are 'localised', that is, they only increase the productivity of inputs in the neighbourhood of the input proportions (and input prices) at which the innovation is made. This may also apply to dynamic economies such as those due to learning by doing. Other factors may inhibit the international transmission of new technologies or products.

Empirical research carried out by Vernon and his associates at the Harvard Business School, by Kenen and his associates at Columbia University, and by others[5] has shown that inter-country differences in technology, research and development expenditures, and product-cycle trade are important in many manufacturing industries. Hufbauer (1966) has analysed world trade in synthetic materials from this point of view. At the more descriptive level the histories of several industries appear to lend support to the product-cycle and technological-gap trade hypotheses. For example, after World War II the US was a large exporter of radio receivers. As the rest of the world, but especially Japanese producers, learnt the technology the US imported large quantities of radios. The trade flow was reversed after the development of transistors by the US. However, the transistor technology also spread abroad and the US again began to import radios. The process was reversed once more after development of printed circuitry. In the electronics component industry the moves from vacuum tubes to transistors, integrated and miniaturised circuits resulted in similar trade patterns. Kindleberger reports on several other case studies including the film-making and office-machine industries (1968, Chapter 4).

INTRA-INDUSTRY TRADE

The preceding model of technological-gap and product-cycle trade was developed without any reference to intra-industry trade. We now need to establish a connection between the two.

[5] See the papers in NBER, 1970, and references therein.

First assume that the product Y in our model is a homogeneous good for which no substitutes are close enough to be reported as trade in the same industrial class. Under these conditions intra-industry trade can appear only if the relevant accounting period encompasses the development or cessation of comparative advantage. This case is of no particular analytical or empirical importance.

Second, let us consider that product Y in our model is one of many close substitutes making up a given industry's spectrum of products differentiated by quality or style. In the extreme and pure case it may be assumed that country A imports a certain proportion of the differentiated goods in the spectrum, including Y, and while it produces some domestically, none are exported during static equilibrium up to time t_0. After the innovation, imports of Y are reduced and, at t_1, exports develop. Between time t_1 and t_3 country A's statistics will show intra-industry trade consisting of the export of Y and the continued import of Y substitutes.

A more realistic model considers industries such as the pharmaceutical industry, where research and development produce a rapid turnover of products most of which dominate previously marketed substitutes or serve specialised requirements existing throughout the world. Most industrialised nations of the world have firms competing in the world-wide market for pharmaceuticals. In this industry (SITC 541), the observed level of intra-industry trade, which was 59 per cent in 1967–8, consists to a large extent of the international exchange of new products protected by patents and copyrights. Other research-intensive industries of this type are the chemical, producers' durable, computer and photographic equipment industries.

However, we now come to an important ambiguity in our analysis of intra-industry trade in Chapter 6, and the role of product-cycle goods. We have argued in the preceding chapter that economies of scale in the form of length of runs may provide the best explanation for intra-industry trade in oligopolistic industries characterised by goods with similar input requirements. It is recalled that the automobile, prepared food and steel industries were outstanding examples of such oligopolies. The product-cycle explanation of trade in these industries is both a rival for and a complement to the economies of scale explanation. In these industries product innovation is an important feature of competition and the cycle of development, output, export and product death or imports can be observed in the dynamic context which the previous chapter's analysis had neglected. Therefore, to the extent that innovations in these industries are protected by copyright and patents, intra-industry trade can be explained by the product cycle even if the goods have identical input requirements and there are no economies of scale. Essentially the identity of input requirements on which our arguments in Chapter 6 are based is only hypothetical and cannot be realised because of the artificial restraints on the flow of knowledge. In this sense the economies of scale and product-cycle explanations of intra-industry trade are rivals.

The two explanations can be considered as complements under the following circumstances. Initially country A produces and imports but does not export any close-substitute products making up the spectrum of differentiated goods of a certain industry. At time t_0 country A develops a new product Y', which is a close substitute to the import good Y. Now assume that Y' is a typical cycle good in the sense that in the absence of legal protection country A would not produce it. The novel item of the analysis enters through the argument that, under the umbrella of initial protection, economies of the type discussed in Chapter 6 develop. We are then back at the point in our analysis of Chapter 6 where, as a matter of comparative statics, we assume the existence of these economies of scale and existing domestic and world relative prices determine the pattern of trade.

One possibility with economies of plant size is that large scale of output of the initial producers may overcome other cost disadvantages and the change from an export good may not be reversed, that is, the cycle is not completed. Another possibility is that product Y may revert to an import good again if country A develops still another substitute, Z, for Y and the demand for Y is diminished but is positive after the availability of Z in country A.

The preceding model, blending the economies of scale and product-cycle analysis, may well embody a realistic explanation of observed intra-industry trade in industries where fashions and styles are important and originate in some large metro-politan centre such as Paris or New York. It has often been noted by travellers and other observers that styles and fashion trends in clothing, food and consumer durables are set in these centres and spread only slowly to the rest of the world, at first involving exports from the centre, later local production and finally exports to the original centre of development. It is highly likely that similar cycles can be found in producers' goods and intermediate products, though in these instances suitability for particular relative factor prices, performance characteristics such as output per time period, quality of output, etc. are the distinguishing features of the product evolution.

The technology-gap and product-cycle models developed so far, fail to provide answers to two important questions. First, the models do not explain why country A produces and exports good Y which has certain style, quality or performance charac-teristics distinguishing it from good X, produced in and exported from the rest of the world. Second, the models do not explain why some countries produce and export cycle and gap goods while other countries do not.

The answer to the first question can be found in our analysis of Chapter 6, which investigated the determinants of quality and style of differentiated products entering intra-industry trade. Presumably country A develops high-quality cycle goods if the income distribution of its population encourages it. Similarly, historically and culturally determined tastes of the domestic population influence the styles of cycle goods that individual countries are likely to develop.

CAPITAL THEORY AND INTRA-INDUSTRY TRADE

The second question raises a more fundamental issue and leads us into an important methodological criticism of the entire product-cycle analysis. In order to create an analytically useful pure case of observed inter-country differences in the propensity to export product-cycle or technology-gap products let us assume that only country A has such exports while the rest of the world has none. The problem then becomes to explain why country A shows this pattern of specialisation.

The critical Heckscher–Ohlin assumption which the product-cycle and technology-gap analysis relaxes concerns the free and instantaneous flow of knowledge among countries which is necessary for the existence of identical production functions in all countries. Undoubtedly it is a useful step towards greater realism to relax this assumption. However, its relaxation does not provide us with an answer to the question we have posed, namely why territory A is the one producing all of the innovations, which, *together with* the assumption about the restricted flow of information, gives us the product-cycle and technology-gap trade.

The explanation can be found in the Fisherian approach to capital theory and its application to international economics.[6] According to this view the traditional factor of production 'capital' consists of three distinct components, physical, human and knowledge capital. Efficiency in the allocation of capital requires that the marginal productivity of all three forms of capital is equal. A second relevant aspect of this view is that there is a market for the commodity knowledge, though because of the public-goods aspect of much knowledge, commercially produced knowledge tends to be embodied in copyrighted or patent-protected new products and technology. Knowledge embodied in this form can be sold and bought like other commodities. The sales provide a return to the investment in knowledge. The third relevant aspect of the theory involves the empirical judgement that knowledge production requires human and real capital-intensive processes.

These three salient features can be combined into an explanation of the technological-gap and product-cycle exports of country A. All we need is the assumption that this country has a favourable overall capital–labour ratio and that it allocates this capital efficiently to the three forms. As a result, the traditional Heckscher–Ohlin model applied in a straightforward manner explains the observed pattern of specialisation. If we assume that capital depreciates and becomes obsolete through the passage of time we can readily generate the cycles of development, exports and imports of the technological-gap and product-cycle goods. However, we shall not present here the detailed application of the traditional model and depreciation since it would lead us too far from our basic topic.

[6] One of the first exponents of this view was Johnson (1963).

The Fisherian approach does not invalidate the technological-gap and product-cycle models but complements them. The capital model has the following favourable aspects. First, empirical studies support the view that the capital-rich country, the United States, exports goods whose production embodies high levels of human capital and research and development expenditures.[7] Second, it can explain the apparent continuous US comparative advantage in goods which are produced by labour-intensive processes, such as for computers and aeroplanes. Third, methodologically, it is more elegant to have explanations of trade patterns which do not require the assumption that artificial barriers prevent the market-determined flow of resources or products, as does the product-cycle and technology-gap analysis.

Fourth, in the real world, there exists the following phenomenon, which the Fisherian approach can explain much more readily than the gap and cycle models. Multinational corporations, which develop their own innovations and are not constrained by patent or copyright laws from shifting production to the lowest-cost country in the world, do not typically do so. We may conclude from this fact that it is the comparative advantage bestowed by the availability of human and knowledge capital which leads to the development and shake-down phases of innovations to be located in the advanced industrial countries. According to this analysis, production function differences between countries based on barriers to knowledge transmission are not even a necessary condition for the existence of technology-gap and product-cycle trade.

Our criticism does not affect the preceding analysis of the cycle illustrated by Fig. 7.1 and the linking of this cycle with the phenomenon of intra-industry trade. Therefore, the heart of this chapter remains valid whether or not ultimately the capital approach will be accepted as the basic explanation of the technological-gap and product-cycle trade.

FOREIGN PROCESSING

The rapid growth of multinational enterprises, which stimulated much of the research on product cycles and technology gaps,

[7] See Keesing (1965, 1966), Hufbauer (1970), Gruber and Vernon (NBER, 1970).

produces the surprising result that, in 1965, 52 per cent of the exports of 320 major US manufacturing firms were to their overseas affiliates. [8] Most important for our present purposes of analysis are the further facts that about one-third of these exports were destined for further processing abroad and that a certain, but unknown, fraction of these goods were reimported into the United States or exported to third countries after this processing.

Helleiner (1973) provides a number of examples of commodities involved in this trade and we shall present some of them here to indicate how it can give rise to the phenomenon of intra-industry trade, the main focus of the present analysis. Thus, Helleiner cites the examples of the assembly of electronic equipment and components, by US and Japanese firms, from imported parts in Hong Kong, Singapore, South Korea, Taiwan and Mexico. Garments, gloves, leather luggage and baseballs are sewn together in the West Indies, south-east Asia and Mexico from components imported from the United States and Japan. Jewels for watches are precision-drilled in Mauritius for Swiss watch-makers. Mexican factories assemble US-supplied ammunition for the United States army. German cameras are assembled in Singapore from German parts.

It is easy to see that these types of labour-intensive assembly or finishing processes give rise to intra-industry trade because in many countries, and at most available aggregation levels, the parts and assembled products are classed in the same statistical category. This fact is most obvious in the case of the electronics industry where the distinction between parts, components and complete products often is blurred, though it also occurs in other industries.

As an example, the US Tariff Commission reports this form of international trade in two import items, items 806.30 and 807.00 of the US Tariff Nomenclature. These items permit import duties to be levied only on the foreign value-added and other non-US-sourced components when some inputs originated in the US. The rate of duty is the rate which would otherwise apply to the total value of the final product. Item 806.30 reports articles of metal and 807.00 other fabricated products made of US components but processed abroad in the manner described above.

[8] See Bradshaw (1969).

US imports in these two categories rose dramatically from $953 million in 1966 to $2211 million in 1970. The dutiable foreign value-added in these imports fell from 84·6 per cent in 1966 to 75·6 per cent in 1970, indicating increased reliance on US components in the assembly process. However, in the case of US trade with developing countries, the dutiable value-added on class 807 imports alone rose from 3·9 per cent in 1966 to 14·3 per cent in 1970 while the share of the developing countries in the class 807 trade rose from 6·8 per cent in 1966 to 24·9 per cent in 1970. These latter developments indicate that multi-national firms are increasing rapidly their use of developing countries' labour in the processing of each good and in the number and value of goods processed.

Helleiner and others have analysed the causes and likely effects of this trade on economic development and world-wide patterns of specialisation. We can use the insights of this analysis to explain how the traditional trade theory needs to be extended or modified to account for the phenomenon of intra-industry trade based on foreign processing. Two such modifications or extensions suggest themselves.

First, we must remember that, in most traditional trade models, services such as hair-cuts, but also finishing and assembly processes, are non-tradable in the conventional sense because they cannot be shipped abroad. In fact, in the case of most services the ratio of transport cost to price approaches infinity. However, it is not difficult to introduce the idea of the tradability of services through embodiment into commodities, as is taking place with the finishing and assembly processes described above.

Yet, not all services are tradable in this sense and certain conditions have to be met before such trade takes place. Thus the costs of transport of the goods must be small enough and the cost of services performed abroad must be low enough that it is profitable not to use domestic substitute services. The examples of electronic equipment and cameras assembled in developing countries seem to meet these requirements very well. These goods possess high value and small bulk, making for low transport costs relative to the price of the product. Relatively simple labour-intensive processes are in fact much cheaper in developing countries than in the developed countries.

The surge of international processing in the last half of the sixties coincided with the dramatic lowering of transport costs and increases in the speed of delivery brought about by modern jet aircraft.

Second, we need to introduce into the traditional models the cost of information about markets for goods, factor supplies, etc. The assembly and finishing processes mentioned above are integral and essential parts of the manufacture and marketing of the goods involved. The maintenance of quality and production schedules in these processes therefore are crucial for the success of the entire business. Such maintenance of quality and production schedules can be assured only through the efficient flow of information and personnel between home countries and the countries in which the processing takes place.

As is well known, the sixties saw the technological development in electronics of cheap and efficient means for the transmission of information; the revolution in jet aircraft has enabled personnel to travel quickly and cheaply. As Kindleberger (1969) has pointed out, these advances in communication and transport technology may well be the ultimate explanation of the rapid growth of the multinational corporations in this era. Taking advantage of these low costs of communication and travel, these corporations market and produce in many countries and it seems to be a natural development that they should use their existing network of information flows to take advantage of the particular profit opportunities arising from international processing.

As a corollary of the efficient information flow we might mention that in most of the developing countries in which international processing takes place local governments provided subsidies and generated other favourable conditions for the development of these kinds of industrial activity. For example, industrial free trade zones and extraterritorial areas with factory buildings and warehouses had to be provided to permit the efficient import, processing and re-export of these goods without the payment of duties and involvement in other bureaucratic red tape. There is little doubt that the multinational corporations provided important information to local governments about the need for and the nature of these activities without which international processing would not have become feasible.

In sum, international assembly and finishing, which give rise to intra-industry trade because they involve the import and export of goods which often are reported in the same statistical category, are consistent with the Heckscher–Ohlin model since they represent the exploitation of comparative advantage in the production of certain services. The new element in the analysis not typically found in the traditional model is that this trade in services takes place through embodiment in real commodities and that it is economic only when costs of transport relative to the value of the good are low enough and when communication and travel are efficient and cheap enough to assure the international integration of the production of goods.

Part III Some Implications for International Trade Theory and Policy

8 Gains from Free or Freer Trade

THE GAINS FROM TRADE

The social gains from trade in the differentiated products which show up in the international trade statistics as intra-industry trade are essentially the same as the gains from trade in homogeneous commodities. In the case of both homogeneous and differentiated commodities, international trade results in an expansion of the production-possibility frontier and a further expansion of the consumption-possibility frontier because of the exchange of goods among nations on terms more favourable than the relative prices of an autarkic nation. In the case of differentiated commodities the precise nature of the gains is more complex in that there is no single cause or model explaining international trade in differentiated commodities. We have developed several alternative models in the previous chapters, each of which gives rise to a particular form of commodity differentiation and international trade. However, in every case, international trade enables the countries to take advantage of the comparative advantage in differentiated commodities which their production possibilities imply. Some brief comments on the gains from trade in some differentiated commodities will serve to explain these gains and introduce the discussion of freeing trade, later in this chapter.

In the case of commodities differentiated by their time or location characteristics the gains are a straightforward extension of the theory of trade in homogeneous commodities. With border trade, there is a reduction in the costs of production and a consequential increase in the consumption frontier of the participating countries when all consumers are supplied from the source with the lowest costs including the costs of transport, regardless of intervening national borders. There is an analogous effect in the case of cycle goods which are exported and imported at different periods of the calendar year. In the case of electricity transmission across borders, a given flow of electricity can be supplied by a smaller generating capacity which is utilised more fully over a 24-hour day if domestic peak-load demands are supplied from abroad and slack-demand periods result in exports of electricity. When the production of internationally traded differentiated commodities takes place either under economies of scale or is due to technological differences there are some additional aspects.

If there are decreasing costs of production the possible welfare gains from international trade are generally greater than under constant or increasing unit costs of production, *ceteris paribus.* Assuming that unit costs of production decrease beyond some level of output rather than remain constant or increase above the initial level, international specialisation which permits larger output and lower unit costs of production will increase the consumption possibilities. For this general argument it does not matter whether the economies are a function of size of plant or length of run. This source of gain is additional to that from trading in commodities in which the relative costs differ among countries but are constant or increasing.[1]

The existence of static economies of scale raises the important question whether the market-induced specialisation pattern is likely to maximise special welfare. In Chapter 3 it was argued that historically determined tastes or incomes may cause a proportionately greater consumption of one commodity, say X, in one country, country A, in the absence of trade and that the existing world price ratio for the closest substitutes to this country's own-produced commodities meant welfare gains from specialisation in X. We abstracted from the question of whether there is a market mechanism which assures that, at any given world price ratio, country A specialises in the production of that good which permits it to reach the highest level of social welfare.

This question can be illustrated by assuming that, initially,

---

[1] In general equilibrium, this can be illustrated by Fig. 6.2. Consider the initial production possibility at point C, of the two goods considered. If there are decreasing costs (increasing returns) to both X and Y in the neighbourhood at C the production-possibility frontier will be convex. It must lie outside the frontier passing through C when there are constant returns to scale in both industries since the latter will be concave to the origin.

after-trade specialisation is in good X at world price WW, as in Fig. 6.2. Now assume that the world price ratio changes through some exogenous influence so that X is now relatively cheaper and the slope of the price line is less than that of the line SW. Continued specialisation in X leads to a level of welfare lower than $I'I'$ and lower than is attainable through specialisation in good Y.

Whether producers in country A are likely to switch to producing Y depends on the nature of the assumed economies of scale. If the increasing returns to scale are internal to the firms the assumed change in the world price ratio causes them to switch from X to Y. This conclusion holds whether the economies of scale are static or whether they are dynamic and due to learning by doing and specialised knowledge creation. According to the generalised capital approach propounded at the end of Chapter 7 these dynamic economies of scale can be considered as being the result of human and knowledge capital formation. The drawing of the production-possibility frontier of Fig. 6.2 assumes that country A can produce either X or Y *after* the appropriate human and knowledge capital formation. Thus the assumed greater profitability of Y relates to the time after these investments have been undertaken by the firm.

It should be noted that the preceding discussion of how an oligopolistic industry reorganises output in response to changes in individual firms' competitiveness represents a rather special model of oligopolistic behaviour. The literature contains numerous models of oligopolistic market behaviour, many of which have solutions with output, market shares, etc. determined randomly or according to game-theory solutions. This book is not the place to review these models.[2] For the analysis of intra-industry trade they have the rather unattractive feature that the indeterminacy of the solution means that little can be said *a priori* about the pattern of international specialisation and the gains from trade. It cannot be ruled out that these models describe the world more accurately than those in which costs of production and consumer tastes determine equilibrium relationships. If this is so, much of the preceding analysis has to be modified in obvious ways.

Moreover, there are likely to be substantial elements of

[2] For a discussion, see Caves (1966).

external economies of scale associated with human and know-ledge capital creation. If the economies are external to the firms in the industries, the changes in the relative product prices may not induce firms to switch from one specialisation to another since, with scarce primary resources, the marginal costs of each firm increase with output. However, recent theorising about the adaptation of market institutions to externalities suggests that firms tend to merge to internalise the external economies or create industry-sponsored agencies for the production of the new human and knowledge capital.[3] In this event they would profit from the new world price ratio. As an example, the Swiss watch industry responded to the challenge of electric wrist watches invented in the United States by creating a research institute whose explicit aim was to develop an electric watch mechanism which avoided the patent protection of the US system.[4]

Another essential ingredient of the analysis of Chapter 3 dealing with the determinants of intra-industry trade in dif-ferentiated products is the market organisation under conditions of imperfect competition. The opening up of trade may give rise to additional welfare gains through changes in market organisation. Welfare losses due to the monopoly in national markets are reduced when international trade increases competition and the number of suppliers in each market. The increase in the number of suppliers of close-substitute goods increases the elasticities of demand for the products of domestic suppliers.[5] This tends to result in a smaller divergence between the market price for the product and the marginal cost of pro-duction and in reduced loss of welfare as conventionally mea-sured by the loss of consumers' surplus. However, this result is not certain. Companies may merge, collude or share markets with the result that national monopolies or oligopolies are replaced by international monopolies or oligopolies.[6] The

[3] For example, Coase (1966).

[4] The search was unsuccessful and an agreement was signed resulting in the Swiss manufacture of electric watches under licence.

[5] It has been argued that there is another and frequently more important source of gain because greater competition in a market may force firms to increase the efficiency of factor use; see Leibenstein (1966) and Comanor and Leibenstein (1969).

[6] Scitovsky (1958) gives some examples in the case of freeing trade through customs unions.

likelihood of any given result is influenced by the strength of national and supranational anti-trust authorities.

The opening of trade may also increase consumer choice. The number of brands offered to consumers increases either because more foreign firms enter the market or because existing firms find it profitable to cater to the special tastes or functional requirements of certain segments of the market through the development of product variants differentiated by brand, style or functional characteristics. Such increases in the number of differentiated products may be made possible as a result of lower average cost of producing each, following the opening up of trade and increased length of runs in all countries. Competition among producers for the increased total demand for the industry's output priced lower on the average takes many forms, one of which may be the launching of new products.

There has been much discussion in the literature as to whether such products differentiation does in fact increase welfare. It has been argued that much of modern product differentiation involves only minor or no improvements in functional characteristics, from which products derive their ultimate usefulness. From this point of view product differentiation results in higher average cost per unit of functional characteristic of each good and therefore it is undesirable.

However, it has also been argued that product differentiation meets the apparently strong public preference for consumption patterns expressing individual taste and style. From this point of view highly differentiated products such as cars of different make and design are considered by consumers to be not only means of transport but also a way of reflecting the owner's status, taste and values. In terms of Lancaster's terminology of goods characteristics which we have used elsewhere, the differentiated product supplies quantities of multiple characteristics which the consumers demand. Product differentiation and advertising do not *create* consumers' basic desire to convey status, taste and values in this manner; they merely supply the characteristics demanded. Furthermore, much product differentiation which appears to be superficial and frivolous to some observers does in fact represent a new combination of performance characteristics which increases the products' usefulness in particular, specialised tasks. According to this view an increase in the number of differentiated products available after the opening of trade represents a clear welfare gain.

The discussion of gains from trade has so far been confined to gains from international trade of final consumer goods. More than one-half of world trade by value is trade in capital goods rather than final consumer goods. While we do not have any quantitative estimates of the proportion of intra-industry trade which consists of trade in capital goods, we cited some evidence in Chapter 3 that some intra-industry trade is trade in materials, components and fixed capital equipment. The exchange of such materials, components and fixed capital equipment between producers in the same industries of two or more countries leads to gains from trade in the form of an outward shift of the production-possibility frontier which are no different to gains from inter-industry specialisation among countries in the production of capital and consumer goods. However, observations of intra-industry specialisation among countries in the exchange of capital goods indicate that the benefits of such international exchanges add to the benefits of nations specialising in the exchange of final consumer goods for other final consumer goods or final consumer goods for capital goods.

It should be noted that the intra-industry share of trade is not an indicator of the welfare gains from trade. The use of intra-industry trade share for this purpose would imply that the gains per dollar of intra-industry trade were greater or less than the gains from inter-industry trade. It has been suggested by Linder (1961, p. 140) and Drèze (NBER, 1970, p. 211) that the gains from trade in primary products or in Heckscher–Ohlin products may be greater than trade in other products, presumably because it is suspected that the pre-trade initial relative cost differences may be greater in the former case. This suggestion neglects the gains from economies of scale, increased competition and consumer choice and the distinction is not the same as that between intra- and inter-industry trade. In any case the notion of gains from trade is a device to indicate the policies that are required to maximise total welfare and it is immaterial whether the gains from one dollar of trade are greater than those from another. Nor is intra-industry trade to be taken as a measure of the extent to which trade is free, although there is substantial evidence that the increases in trade after trade liberalisation have, in recent years, largely taken this form.

The gains from introducing trade which have been outlined above, or slight modifications of them, also apply to liberalising existing trade. We now consider unilateral and then multilateral reductions in levels of protection.

INTRA-INDUSTRY PROTECTION AND TRADE

There is probably a considerable variance in the levels of effective protection for producers of different commodities or commodity groups *within* the manufacturing industries of most countries. However, most studies of effective protection have been confined to making estimates of the rates of effective protection for manufacturing industries which are highly aggregated. In Australia, the Tariff Board recently observed that 'every industry includes some activities requiring only low rates of protection to compete with imports', although the whole manufacturing sector is commonly thought to be import-competing. The Board itself has made some estimates of the distribution of effective rates of protection available within 31 manufacturing industries for the year 1967–8. According to these estimates the dispersion of effective rates among the products of each industry is greater, in many industries, than the dispersion of average rates among the industries themselves. This dispersion of effective rates of protection within industries is, like the observed levels of intra-industry trade, a reflection of the obvious but usually neglected fact that manufacturing industries typically have a comparative advantage in some of the products they produce and a comparative disadvantage in other of their products.[7] This dispersion of effective rates of protection has some obvious implications when we take actual or potential intra-industry trade into consideration.

The relatively high levels of protection of some manufacturing goods within an industry[8] reduces the exports as well as the

[7] The same features may apply of course to non-manufacturing industries.

[8] An industry for this purpose is best defined as a group of producing enterprises but in most cases this classification will correspond closely to commodity groups.

imports of manufactures since they compete directly for the same scarce resources, particularly managerial and skilled labour. Consequently a reduction in the relatively high levels of protection will increase exports as well as imports by the industries concerned. The intra-industry movement of resources as well as the inter-industry movement, upon the reduction of higher rates of protection, lead to an increase in consumer welfare. Moreover, lower average protection in the high-protection areas will encourage producers to produce a smaller range of products but to produce each on a larger scale or in longer production runs and hence to lower unit costs of production.

In addition such intra-industry resource movements have the advantage that they may reduce transitional costs of unemployment and surplus capacity, upon changes in protection. However, they do not necessarily eliminate them completely. An increase in the intra-industry specialisation in production may mean, at one extreme, an increase in the production and exports of a single commodity and an increase in the imports of another single commodity. At the other extreme, it may mean an increase in the production and exports of several of the commodities produced by the industry together with increases in imports of several commodities. Both cases imply an increasing international exchange of commodities and increased specialisation in production but the two cases may have quite different implications for the companies and regions producing the industry's commodities. For example, if in the first case, the one commodity with increasing exports is produced by a group of producers located in a particular region separate from the other producers of the industry, then the exports of this commodity may enable the latter producers to adjust easily to the changes in trade but the other producers may be harmed substantially. On the other hand, the increase in exports may be widely distributed among all producers.

The extent of the adjustments in production which are required by any change in international trade also depend on the share of these traded commodities in the total production of the companies and regions affected. Nevertheless, the movement of resources to other uses within the same industry where job skills and input requirements are similar to those of the earlier use will reduce the time and costs of adjustment.

It should be noted that we may take an observed increase in intra-industry trade after the freeing of some trade to imply an increase in intra-industry specialisation in *production*. An increase in the measure of intra-industry trade used in this study merely means that there has been an increase in the extent to which the total commodity exports and total commodity imports of an industry offset each other. But, provided the total export plus import trade increase,[9] an increase in the percentage of intra-industry trade must mean an increase in intra-industry specialisation in production, although as we noted above, the nature of this specialisation in trade and production may vary significantly.

CUSTOMS UNIONS

The same general points concerning the gains from more trade will apply to customs unions and other regional trading arrangements, with slight modification because of the increase in access to export markets that occurs along with the reduction in the protection of importable commodities and because the reductions in protection are discriminatory and may therefore cause a loss of welfare.[10] One cannot predict the quantitative effects of a customs union on individual industries or national welfare because of the complexities of such a major change but one can make certain qualitative generalisations relating to the whole economy.

To discuss the relevance of intra-industry trade to customs unions it is useful to recall one of the first important generalisations that was developed regarding the welfare effect of a customs union. This is the proposition that the welfare of the union as a whole, and of the world, is greater the more competitive or similar are the member countries in terms of the lists

[9] If total export plus import trade decreases, an increase in the percentage of intra-industry trade does not imply an increase in intra-industry specialisation. For example, in a manufacturing industry with more exports than imports, an increase in import protection may encourage a greater range of goods to be produced, and reduce specialisation and total trade but increase the intra-industry trade.

[10] A piecemeal reduction in tariffs which discriminates among commodities though not among countries may also cause welfare losses in this way.

of tradable commodities produced *before* the union, and the more complementary or dissimilar they are in terms of the spread of production costs of these commodities among member countries. The second part of the criterion implies that the members of the union have different relative factor endowments which under the free trade conditions result in inter-industry specialisation. Consequently the expansion of trade among union members is more likely to be trade-creating and to result in a more efficient location of production than is the case when external union tariffs divert trade from the rest of the world to a less efficient union member. Such gains due to the 'production effects' of the union were proposed for competitive industries producing homogeneous products under constant or decreasing returns to scale.[11]

The theory of intra-industry trade does not invalidate this conclusion but it suggests the following modification. The welfare of the union is the greater the more competitive or similar are the lists of member countries' tradable differentiated goods produced *before* the union and the more the production of these differentiated goods is subject to economies of scale. Reduced trade barriers within the union may lead some firms and plants to specialise more in the production of lines in which they have a cost advantage, as discussed in the previous section. A union between countries with competitive pre-union output and no complementarity of industries after union in the conventional sense, but opportunities for intra-industry specialisation, may result in greater welfare gains than does the union between countries with competitive pre-union output, complementarity in the constant-cost sense, but no opportunities for intra-industry specialisation. Essentially economies of scale and intra-industry specialisation reduce the possibility of net trade diversion to higher-cost sources of supply.[12]

In addition, the theory of intra-industry trade stresses the mutual interpenetration of oligopolistic market structures

[11] The analysis of a customs union should also consider the effects on the pattern of effective rates of protection and relative prices to consumers and terms of trade but little can be said concerning the presence of intra-industry trade and these effects.

[12] For a definition of trade diversion when economies of scale are present, and a discussion of the production effects of a customs union in this context, see Krauss (1972, pp. 420–1, 432–4).

following customs union formation. The advertising campaigns, opening of new sales outlets and organisation of sales forces which accompany the consolidation of product lines and intra-industry specialisation are part of the 'dynamic benefits' from integration discussed by traditional customs unions theory. These benefits, according to the theory of intra-industry trade, tend to result in an overall increased 'efficiency' in the industries surviving after the union. However, a customs union will not reduce monopoly power or increase efficiency within the firm if union-wide oligopolies or monopolies are allowed to replace national oligopolies or monopolies.

Intra-industry trade also has important implications for the short-run costs of adjustment to freeing trade. The emphasis in traditional customs union theory on the expected inter-industry specialisation after the removal of tariff barriers has resulted in an important overestimate of the short-run costs of adjustments and to fears that countries would lose entire branches of manu-facturing industries. For example, when the Benelux Union was negotiated, Belgian textile manufacturers feared being wiped out by the Dutch textile industry known for its low-priced output. In the case of the EEC, French car makers feared serious output losses from German competitors who had been more successful than the French in sales to third countries. The fear of conse-quences of this type are still strong in Canada, where a customs union with the United States is believed widely to reduce Canadians to 'hewers of wood and drawers of water'.[13]

On the other hand, analysis of likely events resulting from customs union formation from the point of view stressed by the theory of intra-industry trade would have predicted that the mutual tariff reduction among countries with similar basic resource endowments, such as the Benelux and the EEC countries and the US and Canada, would result more in intra-industry than inter-industry specialisation. Intra-industry specialisation results in the retention of more industries than under inter-industry specialisation. The losses in the short-run due to the costs of adjustments in output resulting from intra-industry specialisation are reduced but not eliminated.

[13] Wonnacott and Wonnacott (1967, p. 335); for references to similar New Zealand fears in the case of the Australia–New Zealand free trade area, see Lloyd (1971, p. 114).

The extent of adjustment induced by a freeing of trade will depend on several factors: the change in trade, the shares of international trade in production and consumption of traded commodities, and the substitutability of labour and machinery used in the production of the commodities whose total production is reduced for the labour and machinery used in the production of the commodities whose production is expanded. This last factor in turn depends on the similarity of input requirements and the location of the plants which are expanding and contracting. In some cases substantial regional or occupational movements within the industry may be required. In others where the resources are highly substitutable the costs of adjustment may be restricted to minor capital losses of machines which are specific to particular styles or brands of products, and the loss of rent of labour skills specific to particular machines or tasks. We may expect the costs of adjustment to be smaller in the case of a regional trading arrangement than in the case of a unilateral reduction in protection because of the opportunities to expand production for sale in the more open markets of the member countries. Other strategies of adjustment assistance and the maintenance of full employment may also reduce the amount of adjustment induced by the freeing of trade, and the provision of adjustment assistance may redistribute the burden of the costs more equitably among the taxpayers at large.

9 Observed Effects of Trade Liberalisation

Intra-industry trade first came to the attention of international trade economists through observed changes in the pattern of trade after the formation of the European Economic Community. Subsequently other economists have noted that the expansion of trade as a result of the global trade liberalisation measures of the OEEC and GATT in the fifties and sixties and as a result of regional trade arrangements seems to have taken the form largely of an exchange of similar commodities. This chapter re-examines the relationships between the EEC and the growth of intra-industry trade which have received most attention and examines the pattern of trade after the formation of the Central American Common Market and the New Zealand–Australia Free Trade Agreement.

First, we may recall the trend over time in intra-industry trade, which was noted in Chapter 3. Of the changes in the percentage of intra-industry trade for each of the ten developed countries from 1959 to 1964 and again from 1964 to 1967 only two were decreases.[1] Both the Netherlands and Italy experienced slight decreases in the percentages of intra-industry trade, both unadjusted and adjusted between 1964 and 1967 (see Tables 3.1, A3.1 and A3.2). The period 1959–67 was a period of substantial liberalisation of world trade under the auspices of both GATT and the OECD, especially among the industrial countries of the sample. The observed trend is therefore consistent with the

---

[1] The trend in these years is a continuation of a trend, noted by earlier writers, which occurred in the earlier post-World War II years and, before this, in the pre-World War II era. These writers pointed out that the exchange of manufactures for manufactures among the industrial countries of West Europe and North America was increasing in importance and accounted for most of the expansion of trade among these countries (see Chapter 1).

hypothesis that liberalisation increases intra-industry trade as a percentage of total trade as well as absolutely. However, as all the countries experienced substantial liberalisation of trade, this trend does not isolate the effect of trade liberalisation from other possible influences.

The experience of the EEC countries since the EEC began operation on 1 January 1958 gives an indication of the separate influences of trade liberalisation. The measures of intra-industry trade for each of the five members of the EEC, treating Belgium–Luxembourg as one country, for four years (1954, 1959, 1964, 1967) are set out in Tables A9.1 to A9.4. These measures relate to trade with other members of the EEC only. To obtain comparable estimates for these four years it was necessary to compute these measures at the 2-digit level of the SITC rather than the preferred 3-digit level. The years 1959, 1964 and 1967 were chosen in part to coincide with the observations for the same three years of the total intra-industry trade as a percentage of the *total* trade of these countries with all trading partners, which were mentioned in the above paragraph. The year 1954 precedes the formation of the EEC and much of the liberalisation of trade by the OEEC and the European Payments Union. Although the first 10 per cent tariff cut took place on 1 January 1959 it was generally applied to imports from non-member countries, and there was little discrimination against non-members until the second tariff cut on 1 July 1960.

The relationships between the growth of intra-industry trade and total trade may be summarised in the following three observations:

1   Total intra-EEC trade increased more rapidly than the trade of the EEC countries with non-members; the annual compound rates of growth of export trade between 1959 and 1967 were 12·1 per cent and 8·0 per cent respectively.
2   Intra-industry trade as a percentage of the total trade among the EEC member countries rose from 53 per cent in 1959 to 65 per cent in 1967 (Table 9.1).
3   Total intra-industry trade as a percentage of the total trade of the EEC countries *with all trading partners* rose from 44 per cent in 1959 to 53 per cent in 1967 (Table 3.6).

The first observation is consistent with the effects of a discriminatory reduction of tariffs within a customs union or free

trade area.[2] The second observation indicates that much of this
expansion of intra-EEC trade took the form of the increased
exchange of commodities within the 2-digit classes of the
SITC. This observation was first made by Balassa (1963, 1966)
and Grubel (1967).[3] However, neither Balassa nor Grubel
measured intra-industry trade directly. Balassa (1966) reached
the conclusion on the basis of the observed increase in the
uniformity of the commodity export patterns of the EEC
countries and on the basis of an unweighted average measure of
inter-industry trade. Grubel observed the relative shares which
each country held in intra-EEC exports of individual industries
and the ratios of exports/imports or imports/exports, whichever
was the greater, of an industry. The fall in the variance of the
former shares and the movement towards unity of the latter
ratios were taken as evidence of increasing intra-industry
specialisation. Both Balassa and Grubel examined trade in
manufactures only.

In Tables A9.1 to A9.4 the increase in the share of intra-
industry trade in the intra-EEC trade of the member countries
is measured directly for the first time. These tables show that
the shares rose steadily from 53 per cent in both 1954 and 1959
to 65 per cent in 1964 and 66 per cent in 1967. The increase of
the share of intra-industry trade between 1959 and 1967
coincides with the period of lowering tariff barriers within the
EEC. The percentage of the *increase* in trade which was intra-
industry trade between 1959 and 1967 has been calculated
exactly in Table 9.1. The data in this table reveal that 70·9 per
cent of the increase in total trade among the EEC countries over
this period took the form of an increase in intra-2-digit-industry
trade.

There is an interesting test of the hypothesis that the increases
in international trade which result from trade liberalisation are

---

[2] It could, alternatively, be due at least in part to the relatively rapid
growth of the EEC economies and their growing dominance of world
markets for many commodities, some of which may be independent of the
formation of the EEC and the effects of this itself on the growth of member
countries. For this view, see Major (1962).

[3] Earlier, Verdoorn (1960) had observed the same tendency towards
intra-industry trade within the Benelux countries after the formation of
that customs union. His evidence was the reduced dispersion of the export–
import ratios.

TABLE 9.1
Intra-Industry and Total Trade Among EEC Countries, 1959 and 1967
($US million)

	1959			1967		
	Intra-Industry Trade	Total Trade		Intra-Industry Trade	Total Trade	
Belgium–Luxembourg	1,920·1	3,025·5	63·5	6,137·9	8,425·3	72·9
Netherlands	1,758·0	3,073·6	57·2	5,679·0	8,550·3	66·4
Republic of Germany	2,499·6	4,972·0	50·3	8,969·8	14,577·8	61·5
France	1,695·4	2,856·5	59·4	7,316·5	10,074·2	71·6
Italy	626·4	1,682·7	37·2	4,166·1	6,762·8	61·6
Total	8,499·5	15,610·3	54·4	32,269·3	48,390·4	66·7

Notes
1 Total intra-industry trade for a country j is
$$\sum_i [(X_{ij} + M_{ij}) - |X_{ij} - M_{ij}|]$$
2 The averages in columns 3 and 6 are unadjusted averages.
3 The averages for all countries in the last row are equivalent to the mean of all countries, weighting each country by its share of total trade among all EEC countries.
4 The intra-industry trade and total trade statistics were computed from the 2-digit OECD statistics and omit small and insignificant values of confidential trade in nuclear products, etc.

intra-industry rather than inter-industry trade. This test is to compare the share of intra-industry trade in the expansion of the trade among the EEC countries with the corresponding share in the expansion of their total trade with all other countries. The latter share for the same period of 1959 to 1967 is 60·0 per cent of the expansion of the trade of the EEC countries with all trading partners, compared to 70·9 per cent for intra-EEC trade. This is consistent with the hypothesis of greater intra-industry specialisation within the EEC than in the trade of the EEC countries with other countries. We cannot be certain that this has occurred, because of two complications. First, the change within the EEC has been measured at the 2-digit level whereas that of the EEC countries with the rest of the world in Tables 3.1, A3.1 and A3.2 has been measured at the 3-digit level.[4] Second, over this period, the trade of the EEC countries with non-EEC countries has also benefited from substantial freeing of trade as a result primarily of GATT negotiations, and in part from the adjustments of tariffs in the EEC to the Common External Tariff. These adjustments involved some reduction in duties, particularly in France and Italy which had high initial tariffs.[5]

The increase in intra-industry trade which accompanied the formation of the EEC is not in doubt, and the discussion above suggests that the increase in the intra-industry share of total intra-EEC trade is due in part to the formation of the EEC itself and in part to other trade liberalisation. Balassa (1966) and Grubel (1967) took the increase in intra-industry trade, and the associated increases in the uniformity of country's export patterns and shares of each country in the total intra-EEC exports of individual industries, as evidence of greater intra-industry specialisation in production and attributed these to the formation of the EEC. They then interpreted this increasing specialisation as specialisation in differentiated products due to greater economies of scale and length of production run and relative factor-price differences.

Certainly the increase in intra-industry trade contradicted the usual predictions which were derived from identifying the multiproduct industries at the 2- or 3-digit level of the SITC (or ISIC) with the industries of the Heckscher–Ohlin model of international trade. In Balassa's words: 'According to the familiar textbook exposition, multilateral reductions in duties

[4] This difference in the level of aggregation means that we cannot compare the share of intra-industry trade in intra-EEC trade of Tables A9.2 to 9.4 to the shares of intra-industry trade in the trade of the EEC countries with all trading partners of Table A3.1 and Table 3.6. The higher percentages of intra-industry trade within the EEC than in the total trade of EEC countries, in 1959, 1964 and 1967, could be due to either the more aggregative 2-digit statistics or the effects of freer trade within the EEC. However, the difference in level of aggregation is less important when looking at trends in the two series.

[5] We may recall, from Table 3.5, that the percentage increase in the intra-industry trade measures over the period 1959–67 for the EEC countries as a group was actually less than the increase for the other OECD countries.

would lead to a reallocation of resources from import-competing to export industries, accompanied by a contraction in the activity of the former and an expansion of the latter . . . tariff reductions would be followed by inter-industry specialisation, the validity of this hypothesis requires that within each industry the largest supplier, or suppliers, of the preintegration period have the lion's share of the expansion of intra-area trade' (Balassa, 1966). This did not occur. In retrospect, these predictions look very naive. The presence of significant intra-industry trade before the formation of the EEC indicates that even at that time there were no 'export industries' and 'import-competing industries'. In multiproduct industries, comparative costs must be specified in terms of individual commodities and not industries.

Moreover, the great increase in the absolute amount of trade and in intra-industry trade, as recorded in Table 9.1, imply that the intra-industry specialisation in the pattern of international exchange of commodities must also have been accompanied by an increase in the intra-industry specialisation in the patterns of production in the member countries. Unfortunately it is much more difficult in all countries to obtain the detailed data on production and costs than it is to obtain the data on international trade which has been used to calculate the observed measures of intra-industry trade. It is difficult, therefore, to distinguish the particular kind of intra-industry trade and specialisation which has occurred.

Adler (1970) has analysed the relationship between observed changes in the pattern of production and observed changes in the pattern of intra-industry trade in the case of ten steel products in which trade was liberalised by the formation of the European Coal and Steel Community (ECSC) in 1952. He observed that intra-industry trade increased over the period 1954–66[6] and found that, over the same period, the variances of each country's shares of the total Community's export and production of the ten steel products increased for the five member countries. This provides 'reasonably strong evidence of increasing intra-industry specialisation [in production] in the ECSC' (Adler, 1970, p. 179). His evidence suggests that steel

[6] Adler used the Balassa measure of the share of inter-industry trade. A measure of intra-industry trade is obtained simply by subtracting the figures in Adler's Table I from unity.

production as a whole did not concentrate in any single country but that intra-industry specialisation was incomplete. No country specialised completely in one or two steel products, nor did production of any single good concentrate in one country. Furthermore, Adler explained the resulting pattern of partial specialisation in terms of the technological advantage that the Netherlands obtained from its earlier adoption of the basic oxygen furnace, the qualities of steel produced in different countries due to particular ores and smelting methods (e.g. France's specialisation in rolled wires and Belgium's in hot strips and bands) and differences in relative factor prices (e.g. Italy's cheap hydroelectricity). The importance of technological differences in smelting methods exemplifies the technological-gap trade discussed in Chapter 7.

Empirical evidence that regional trading arrangements increase the share of intra-industry trade has also been produced by Willmore (1970) for the Central American Common Market (CACM) and by Lloyd (1971) for trade between Australia and New Zealand. Unlike regional trading arrangements among other developing countries the CACM was very successful in its formative years. The General Treaty of 1960 established the Common Market and by June 1966 had led to the removal of nearly all barriers to trade among the members: Guatemala, El Salvador, Honduras, Nicaragua and Costa Rica. Intra-regional imports at current prices rose from \$29 million in 1959 to \$259 million in 1967. In constant 1963 prices the growth was only slightly less rapid: from \$29 million to \$204 million. The share of manufactures in this trade rose from 42 per cent in 1959 to 70 per cent in 1967.

Willmore examined the changes in the pattern of intra-CACM trade over the period 1959 to 1967 for some 59 commodities from Sections 5–8 of their trade classification, i.e. manufactures other than food products. (This is roughly the 3-digit level of the SITC.) By measuring the correlation coefficients between the commodity exports to other CACM members for pairs of countries, in different years, he concluded that the export patterns of the member countries became more uniform. He also calculated the Balassa measure of inter-industry trade for these 59 industries. Subtracting these figures from unity, we obtain a measure of the share of intra-industry trade in total intra-CACM trade in manufactures, with each industry weighted equally. The shares are reported in Table 9.2.

These data show that intra-industry trade among the developing countries of the CACM is substantial and increased rapidly after the formation of the CACM. The share of intra-industry

TABLE 9.2
Share of Intra-Industry Trade in Manufactures Traded Among CACM Countries (%)

Country	1961	1967
Guatemala	30	53
El Salvador	42	49
Honduras	16	23
Nicaragua	13	32
Costa Rica	19	42
Unweighted mean	22	40

Source: Calculated from data in Willmore (1970, Table 4).

trade within the Common Market for manufactures is possibly not less than the corresponding share for the EEC countries in the same year, 1967. Table A9.4 shows that the average for the 2-digit industries for all the EEC countries within Sections 5, 6, 7 and 8 were 77, 73, 75 and 65 per cent respectively. Moreover, the EEC averages are measured for only 28 industries compared to the 59 used by Willmore and are therefore higher than the averages for the corresponding 59 industries.

Willmore interprets these movements in the commodity pattern of exports and inter-industry trade shares as evidence in support of his thesis that the adjustment of manufacturing industries to the integration of the markets of the CACM took the form of intra-industry specialisation in production. In his view, his thesis is strengthened by the observation that the share of intra-industry trade for Consumer goods industries in 1967 was higher than the share for Intermediate goods industries: 48 per cent compared to 38 per cent.[7] He believed product

[7] Willmore's coverage in these two categories did not exhaust the 59 industries. His analysis is in terms of inter-industry trade rather than the complementary intra-industry trade shares. The figures in the text have been calculated from his Table 7.

differentiation to be higher among consumer goods than among capital goods, and buyers of consumer goods to be less well informed, more conscious of style and brand names and more susceptible to persuasive advertising.

One of the present authors (Lloyd, 1971) has commented briefly on intra-industry trade and the New Zealand–Australia Free Trade Agreement which came into effect on 1 January 1966. Intra-industry trade as a percentage of the bilateral trade between Australia and New Zealand is higher than that between Australia and any of its trading partners, at all levels of aggregation from 7- to 1-digits of the Australian trade classification (see Table 4.1).[8] At the 3-digit level of the SITC 30·5 per cent of the trade between Australia and New Zealand in 1968–9 was intra-industry trade, compared to the next highest figure of 17·6 per cent of the trade between Australia and Canada. This is consistent with the finding noted earlier in this chapter that intra-industry trade was a higher percentage of the intra-EEC trade than of the trade of the EEC countries with non-members of the EEC. However, in the Australia–New Zealand case it cannot be attributed to the free trade provisions of the New Zealand–Australia Agreement. In 1968–9 the free trade items on Schedule A of the Agreement accounted for only 51·5 per cent of the total trade between the two countries. This percentage is not significantly higher than the percentage accounted for by the goods included in this Schedule for the years before the formation of the Agreement. This Agreement is only a partial free trade agreement, the major items included in the free trade provisions being forest products, frozen foods and other selected manufactures.[9] The author concluded that the relatively high level of intra-industry trade between the two members 'may reflect in part the preferences extended by New Zealand to Australia, and vice versa, under the 1933 Trade Agreement which were incorporated in NAFTA but it is more

[8] The measures of bilateral intra-industry trade discussed here were calculated as part of the pattern of intra-industry trade of Australia which has been discussed in Chapter 4. The statistics cited in the text are adjusted for the aggregate bilateral trade imbalance. No figures are available for New Zealand's intra-industry trade with her other trading partners.

[9] The nature of the Agreement and its effects are discussed more fully in Lloyd (1971).

probably the result of the natural advantages which each country has in the markets of the other compared to other countries because of lower transport costs, more frequent shipping services, and more frequent commercial contacts' (Lloyd, 1971, p. 48).[10]

All the authors cited in this chapter who have studied the effects of trade liberalisation on intra-industry immediately recognised that specialisation within industries has important implications for the extent of the adjustment that companies and their employees will be required to make, upon the freeing of trade in industries with prospects for intra-industry specialisation. However, as noted in Chapter 8, the extent of this gain from specialisation within industries depends on the particular commodities which a country's producers can produce efficiently and the location of their plants. The experience of the EEC and EFTA suggests that the adjustments required when intra-industry specialisation predominates are not a major obstacle to trade liberalisation.

[10] Lloyd reported one other finding which is relevant to the possibilities of intra-industry specialisation, namely, that 'there are no export industries in the manufacturing sector in the sense of industries in which all or most companies are much more export-oriented than companies in other industries. In all six [sample] industries there are some firms which export a higher proportion of their output than the average for all companies in all six industries. In fact the variances of export shares among companies in the sample is greater within the six industries than it is between industries. An industry which exports a higher proportion of its total output than the average for the manufacturing sector as a whole is usually one in which a higher proportion of companies is relatively export-oriented rather than one in which all companies export a higher proportion of their total output than is true for the whole manufacturing sector' (Lloyd, 1971, pp.31–2).

10 Economic Policies

In this chapter we shall discuss briefly the policy implications flowing from our theoretical and empirical study of intra-industry trade. As can be seen from the subheadings of this chapter, our study has policy implications for some of the important issues which have faced national governments in the sphere of international economic relations in the past and are most likely to face them in the future.

TRADE LIBERALISATION AND INTEGRATION

As we have stressed in Chapters 8 and 9, trade liberalisation in the European Economic Community, the European Coal and Steel Community and the Central American Common Market resulted in greater trade expansion and fewer adjustment problems than had been anticipated by analysts who had based their predictions on the more traditional model of inter-industry specialization. From these findings it follows that governments interested in promoting freer trade for the benefits of consumers, either through integration or the mutual lowering of tariffs, may be able to overcome opposition to such trade liberalization from producers, workers and other interest groups by two sets of policies.

First, governments should engage in educational programmes aimed at affected industry and at labour likely to be affected by lower tariffs. They should point to the coexistence of exporting and import-competing commodities under protection which are produced by firms and plants within the same industry and they should explain the kind of adjustments that intra-industry trade specialisation implies. We have documented the existence of such industries in Canada, Australia, New Zealand and the ECSC in the preceding two chapters (see also Wonnacott and

Wonnacott (1967), Commonwealth of Australia (1969), Lloyd (1971) and Adler (1970), respectively). There is little doubt that analogous information could be gathered in many countries and for many industries once the focus of empirical studies of this kind had been made available to statisticians and analysts.

Second, the educational policy holding out the prospect of relatively easy adjustment following trade liberalisation should be backed up by the government's willingness to provide adjustment assistance. General adjustment assistance was one of the main features of the US Congressional action leading up to the historic Kennedy Round of tariff negotiations but little assistance has actually been provided.[1] While it is a complex question to decide precisely the criteria which should be used in the provision of adjustment assistance it seems rather clear that criteria based on the traditional concept of inter-industry specialisation may well discourage the socially more efficient intra-industry specialisation.

Such a situation could arise if public adjustment assistance were provided only if factors of production move into a new 'industry', and withheld if factors move into a new specialisation within the same industry. The latter kind of adjustment typically does not result in unemployment in the traditional sense and the case for assistance would be correspondingly reduced. Yet such intra-industry reallocation of resources also involves private costs to the factors involved, even if they are much lower than those involved in the shift to a new industry. On the other hand, if public assistance pays for all private costs of moving to a new industry, factors are encouraged to seek employment in a different industry because it is privately more profitable to do so, even though the social cost of this shift may be higher than reallocation within the same industry.

To the extent that adjustment assistance in conjunction with trade liberalisation in the US and elsewhere is administered in the manner we have suggested, our analysis of intra-industry specialisation therefore implies different criteria for the determination of grants and loans.

[1] For a review of adjustment assistance programmes in the US, Canada and the UK, and of the principles on which the assistance should be based, see Mathews (1971).

DEVELOPMENT STRATEGIES

Development planners and critics of import substitution policies have often made the point that the economies of most developing nations are too small to exhaust the economies of scale associated with many industries, such as steel, automobiles and electronics. For this reason they have recommended the establishment of regional production facilities which would serve a number of countries and a market large enough for the exploitation of economies of scale. This objective is to be accomplished through locating the industry in one developing country and assuring duty-free access of the industry's output in all countries of the region. The individual industries are located in different countries so as to assure an equitable distribution of employment gains and the avoidance of intra-regional balance of payments problems.

One of the main reasons why this apparently sound development strategy has not been successful is that countries cannot agree on the geographical distribution of the industries being considered. The failure to reach such agreement can be blamed on economic nationalism and differences in the prestige and real or perceived growth prospects associated with the industries being proposed for development. A fundamental notion is that if a country does not initially obtain, say, a steel industry, it could never expect to catch up with its neighbour and would forever forgo the prestige and economic advantages associated with having a national steel industry.

The analysis of intra-industry specialisation in this book suggests that many difficulties in the pursuit of integrated regional development of industries could be avoided by the realisation that plants, processes and products making up an 'industry', such as the steel industry, are extremely heterogeneous and that substantial economies of scale are available in the production of many important product lines. Blast-furnaces, rolling-mills for sheet metal, wires, structural steels, the production of specialty steel alloys, the fabrication of intermediate iron and steel products, all can be considered as being separate 'industries' within the broader, conventional definition of the 'steel industry'. We have shown in Chapter 8 that Australia simultaneously exports and imports many iron and steel products which are close substitutes in production. Evidence relating to other countries and industries has been supplied elsewhere in this book. We have interpreted this intra-industry trade as being the result of economies of scale due to the length of runs and other savings from specialisation in relatively narrow product lines.

Moreover, Chapter 7 noted the possibilities of vertical intra-industry specialisation. Multinational corporations operating in many industries are known to have developed narrow specialisation of production in different countries. The out-standing examples are the multinational car companies such as Ford and General Motors, which have located the manufacture of transmission engines, steering equipment, etc. in different countries, which supply these components to assembly lines throughout the world, often to be built into different styles of cars. Furthermore, the risk of world-wide breakdown of operations through strikes and other forces closing individual national plants is being met by having identical products manufactured in more than one country. This last strategy may or may not reduce the gains from specialisation, depending on the size of the company's world-wide demand for the finished product and the precise economies to be had from specialisation. The opportunity to reduce the effects of uncertainty through international diversification of production is, of course, one of the sources of strength of the multinational corporations and is certain to stimulate their further growth.[2] Their successful pursuit of the strategy is evidence of the availability of economies of the kind we have stressed in our analysis of intra-industry trade.

In terms of concrete policies, the preceding analysis implies that countries should seek ways of developing well-specified narrow product lines – such as shoes, shirts, wires, time-pieces – of certain quality, style and performance character-istics, while permitting the import free, or under much lower protection, of other commodities of the same industries. As another example, policies towards automobile assembly and the

---

[2] For a study of the world's car industry, see Baranson (1969). See Caves (1971) for the more general analysis of the nature of multinational corporations and for other examples of gains from such international specialisation.

production of car parts should encourage integration of country's facilities into the global network of specialisation rather than encourage the non-economic proliferation of assembly lines and of domestically produced styles, brands and qualities.

If our interpretation is correct, regional development strategy should permit all countries to have each of the prestigious and basic industries such as steel and electronics, but with the important difference that each country will produce only a relatively small number of products of each 'industry'. Such a strategy should remove many of the obstacles to regional agreement, especially since future growth in markets and the development of skills tend to facilitate the ready addition of product lines in every country.

The regional development strategy just suggested will initially be somewhat more costly than locating the whole industry in one country because a fully integrated industrial complex consisting of a number of optimally sized plants each producing a narrow range of products is likely to yield additional economies not available to a geographically scattered set of optimally sized plants producing the same mix of output. However, our analysis of intra-industry trade, and the regional scattering of plants in developed countries with large markets, suggest that these additional gains from conglomeration are relatively small and, in cases where congestion and pollution problems develop, can even be negative.

On the level of national rather than regional development strategy, the theory of intra-industry trade emphasises the need for individual countries to attempt the concentration of industrial output on narrow product lines in which they have a comparative advantage that may be traced to cultural or historic reasons (see Chapter 6). In industries where such sources of advantage do not exist, conscious efforts should be made to create them. Such a strategy of specialisation and the world-wide exports of narrow product lines of individual industries is distinctly different from the traditional strategy which attempts to replace by domestic production most or all imports of consumer or capital goods, regardless of combinations of quality or style or other functional characteristics. It will be recalled that as a result of such policies the cost of producing all products

are raised because of the shortening of the
...d the increased scarcity of factors of production
...ire industry. Our analysis has shown that even
...ed countries do not produce the full range of
...st industries and that intra-industry special-
...al.

...olicy recommendations are new. However, we
believe that they are worth restating here because our study of
intra-industry trade has produced further empirical evidence
directly supporting them and has shown that even the most
highly industrialised nations benefit from intra-industry trade
in differentiated products.

FOREIGN INVESTMENT AND ANTI-TRUST POLICIES

In recent years foreign investment and multinational corporations have come under increasing criticism from nationalists
and other interest groups of several countries, such as France,
Canada, Australia and many of the developing countries.
Governments in these countries have found it increasingly
difficult to resist public pressures for the imposition of some
limits on the freedom of foreign investors. The causes of these
developments are complex and cannot be reviewed here at the
length they deserve. In the present context we shall limit our-
selves to the discussion of some aspects of the foreign-investment
arguments related to the phenomenon of intra-industry trade.

Most of its recent critics welcome the resources and technology that foreign investment makes available to the host
country. The critics are dissatisfied with the fact that it takes
the form of direct investment, which is alleged to provide
foreigners with undesirable levels of control over the host
countries' factor markets, natural resources and, very important,
the pattern of final consumption. The control over consumption
patterns is considered to be undesirable because the foreign
investors tend to disregard domestic cultural traditions, and
internationalise tastes and eliminate national identity through
advertising and product styling. Moreover, such taste creation
is considered by many critics to be associated with the social
wastefulness of monopolistic competition and other excesses of
capitalist societies.

Analyses of the foreign-investment problem along these lines have been provided by Levitt (1970) and Watkins (1968) for Canada and Servan-Schreiber (1969) for Europe. Levitt and Watkins conclude that the solution to the problem lies in the restriction of foreign ownership of domestic means of production.

The most obvious reply to this policy recommendation is that restriction of foreign investment is a second-best solution to the alleged excesses of monopolistic and oligopolistic competition. As Johnson (1970) has pointed out, market imperfections and distortions are eliminated most efficiently by policies dealing with them directly. Our analysis of intra-industry trade suggests that such restrictions may come at a high cost, for a number of reasons.

First, restriction of ownership is likely to cause a loss of all the resources which would have been transferred through the direct investment since most of the direct investment in oligopolistic markets is not motivated by 'high returns' in the classical manner by lending through bonds, etc., but is motivated by the availability of other sources of comparative advantage which lead indirectly to higher returns from direct foreign investment. As Caves (1971) has argued, these sources of advantage for multinational firms arise from styling and technical development of products, advertising, brand identification, superior management, research, etc. All these features are produced under conditions of increasing returns to scale (short-run marginal cost of using them is near-zero). For a number of reasons beyond the scope of the present analysis, firms are unwilling or unable to develop a market for these sources of comparative advantage and, therefore, if they cannot exploit them through direct foreign investment under their control, they will forgo foreign ownership altogether. The country imposing ownership restrictions thus loses the resources brought into the country by the foreign investors.

Second, direct foreign investment tends to be accompanied by increased competition for local factors of production and fiercer competition in product markets than is common when foreigners compete in local oligopolistic markets only through imports. Competition of this sort tends to disrupt oligopoly agreements and to lower product prices and improve the quality and variety of available products, thus causing direct increases in consumer welfare. These public benefits will be lost if foreign direct investment is prohibited.

Benefits may also be lost if competition in domestic oligopolistic markets through direct foreign investors is prevented by collusive agreements including both foreign and domestically owned firms. For these reasons, governments should attempt to control oligopolies by the proper laws and especially through the maintenance of a threat through further competition from abroad. In the case of some large world-wide oligopolies, collusion may be preventable only through international agreements among sovereign nations.

MERCANTILIST POLICIES

The subsidisation of manufacturing exports through currency undervaluation and direct measures such as grants, tax concessions, etc. is considered to be irrational if it leads to persistent balance of payments surpluses and the accumulation of excessive international reserves. German and Japanese balance of payments during the sixties were strongly and persistently in surplus and were considered by many analysts as signalling the start of a neo-mercantilist period.

Mercantilism had been the main feature of foreign economic policies of governments in the sixteenth to nineteenth centuries in Western Europe. It had come under heavy attack by Adam Smith, John Stuart Mill, David Ricardo and others, and today's conventional wisdom is that mercantilism is irrational and diminishes the surplus country's welfare.

Our analysis of intra-industry trade raises the possibility that mercantilism may not be a completely irrational policy. This conclusion rests on the documented strength of trade in differentiated products. It is very important in our interpretation that economies of scale in production are responsible for this trade. If these economies are in fact important one can interpret the undervaluation of the Deutschmark and Japanese yen during the sixties as a method of encouraging exports to obtain economies which lowered average costs of production below what they would have been in the absence of these policies. Persistent undervaluation under the particular conditions, especially the constraints on capital formation and the time-consuming process of opening new market outlets, may have been necessary for the full exploitation of these economies. As a result of the fall in costs of production it is possible that German and Japanese welfare increased despite the disequilibrium and the accumulation of foreign financial obligations whose liquidity plus interest yield was below the economy-wide productivity of real resources. At the same time the rest of the world has gained through the availability of lower-cost German and Japanese products during this period.

We offer the preceding analysis and conclusions with some reluctance because they are based on rather indirect evidence on the existence and importance of economies of scale and because the policy recommendations following from them lend themselves easily to abuse. In practice it will be nearly impossible to distinguish balance of payments policies inducing surpluses for the sake of gaining employment (beggar-thy-neighbour policies), maintaining surpluses to avoid the domestic political costs of currency revaluations and the genuine case of undervaluation for the sake of enjoying economies of scale in the export sector. Nevertheless the conclusions about the rationality of mercantilist policies we have presented above follow logically from our analysis of intra-industry trade and the existence of economies of scale.

POSTWAR US BALANCE OF TRADE AND PRODUCTIVITY GROWTH

The deterioration of the US balance of trade during the fifties and sixties has been caused by a complex set of developments involving the possible initial undervaluation of some important currencies, changes in protection, especially those resulting from the formation of the EEC, differential rates of income, domestic price and productivity changes, etc. This study is not the appropriate place for a review of the empirical evidence which has been accumulated on this matter. However, one outstanding feature of econometric estimates of income and price elasticities of US foreign trade (see Houthakker and Magee (1969), Gregory (1971)) has been the finding of a persistent deterioration of the US competitive position not accounted for by changes in prices and incomes. Furthermore, studies of productivity trends during the postwar era show relatively greater growth in labour productivity in countries other than the United States. Large unexplained residuals in the sources of productivity gains remain after account has been taken of investment in physical, human and knowledge capital (see Dennison (1962)).

Our analysis of intra-industry trade suggests an interesting explanation for these observed trends. The United States entered the postwar era with *per capita* incomes and markets for manufactured products in oligopolistic industries which were sufficiently large to exhaust most of the potential economies of scale. Even if these had not been exhausted, the potential for further gains was relatively much smaller than that of the major countries of Western Europe and Japan, which entered the era with small domestic markets due to lower *per capita* incomes and smaller populations. At the same time protectionist policies and exchange restrictions in these countries limited access to foreign markets. This initial situation was followed by the lowering of trade barriers generally, falling costs of transport, the special removal of restrictions accompanying the formation of the EEC and EFTA, and a general growth in *per capita* incomes. All these developments permitted industries in countries other than the United States to increase intra-industry specialisation and to enjoy the gains in productivity which we have emphasised in Part II of this book. In Chapter 9 we have documented the growth in intra-industry trade among member countries of the EEC.

We conclude from these facts that one important source of the observed differences in the productivity trends in the United States and abroad during the fifties and sixties has been the greater benefits from more economies of scale through intra-industry specialisation abroad than have occurred in the United States. The decrease in US competitiveness not reflected in price changes can similarly be explained, at least in part, by the development of intra-industry trade if one remembers the following outstanding characteristic of oligopolistic markets. In these markets competition occurs not only through changes in product prices, but also through product innovation, improvement, advertising and other methods not reflected in the unit price indices used in econometric studies. Therefore, if foreign producers during the period under consideration improved the quality of their products and services more rapidly than did the United States, US competitiveness in world markets would have deteriorated even if relative price indices had shown no change or gains to the United States. This deterioration of competitiveness would have manifested itself primarily through increased US imports of consumer goods of oligopolistic industries, since the US exports in these classes of goods have always been relatively small.

In terms of concrete policies, the preceding analysis implies that the United States should face up to the need for a periodic dollar devaluation unless other technological and price trends compensate for the effect of quality improvements accompanying differential rates of economic growth. It may also be noted that in all likelihood Japan and Western Europe will suffer from similar adverse trends in their competitiveness as the now developing nations of the world begin to enjoy the gains from intra-industry specialisation.

11 Some Possible Empirical Tests of Intra-Industry Trade

In the present chapter, we present some ideas about possible empirical studies of the intra-industry phenomenon which would further appreciation of its magnitude and would constitute a verification of theoretical models presented in Part II. We have not been able to make more than the most preliminary explorations of the studies we shall propose. However, we feel that the ideas are worth presenting at this point in the hope that researchers working on other subjects may have assembled particularly relevant analytical tools or data which would enable them to carry out the proposed tests with a minimum of further investments now or in the future. Our discussion is broken into three parts, grouping together research topics extending the kind of measurement of the phenomenon we carried out in Part I of this book, suggesting tests for the grouping of industries into classes of border, cycle, Heckscher–Ohlin and differentiated-product trade, and lastly, predicting the commodity composition of intra-industry trade.

EXTENSIONS OF THE MEASUREMENT OF THE PHENOMENON

In Part I, we measured the strength of intra-industry trade at the 3-digit level of aggregation for a number of countries, at a moment in time and over a nine-year period, and investigated its strength as a function of aggregation in a case study of Australia. The evidence we have accumulated can profitably be extended by the study of:

1 Different countries at the 3-digit level, including developing and socialist countries.
2 Different time periods, especially some extending before World War II and possibly into the nineteenth century and including periods of industrialisation of the West.

3 More cases of intra-industry trade as a function of aggregation.

4 Case studies of individual industries with particularly large levels of intra-industry trade.

Studies of this type should be possible since international trade statistics are fairly readily available in the form required and the technique of measurement is well developed. The ultimate objective of such studies would be to show the extent to which the phenomenon of intra-industry trade depends on statistical aggregation procedures rather than significant economic forces transcending the classification problem.

BASIC CLASSIFICATION OF INDUSTRIES

Our theoretical analysis suggests that it should be possible to distinguish the four analytically pure types of industries: Heckscher–Ohlin, border trade, cycle goods and functionally differentiated products. We would like to suggest a method for the identification of each class of industries through the analysis of trade matrices. We have been unable to specify such a method of identification with sufficient rigour to permit use of the computer, even abstracting from the problems associated with hybrid industries, but we believe that the possibilities for the specification of such a method, and the potential for its use on interesting problems, are large enough to warrant reporting of our preliminary progress.

The data on which the analysis is based consists of published matrices of international trade flows among numbers of countries arranged alphabetically (or according to some other arbitrary criterion) along the rows and columns. These matrices report dollar values of trade at the 3-digit SITC level for a calendar year. Reading across each row we find exports from country i to countries $j, j = 1, 2, \ldots n$. The columns in turn show country i's imports from the other n countries. All matrices for different industries in their published form look similar with apparently random entries and empty cells. The principle of analysis we are suggesting involves the reordering of countries in the rows and columns to produce particular patterns of matrix elements.

For the pure Heckscher–Ohlin types of industries, we expect

to find that countries are either exporting or importing the good, but they are not doing both simultaneously. Consequently, it is possible to rearrange the order of countries in such a way that we obtain a partitioned matrix like the one shown in Fig. 11.1.

Figure 11.1
Reordered Matrix of Trade in Pure H.O. Good

Exports to	Countries							
Imports from	1	2	.	g	h	.	.	n
Country 1	—				×	×	×	×
2		—			×	×	×	×
.			—		×	×	×	×
g				—	×	×	×	×
h					—			
.						—		
.							—	
n								—

In this matrix we have countries $1, \ldots g$ represented as the producers and exporters of the pure H.O. good (say uncut diamonds), while countries $h, \ldots n$ are only importers and users of the good. Consequently the world matrix which groups countries in this manner should show positive entries only in an off-diagonal rectangular submatrix as illustrated in Fig. 11.1. All remaining elements are empty. Of course, even within the rectangle, not all elements must have positive entries since it is not necessary that every producing country exports to all non-producing ones. Furthermore, there may be subgroups of countries yielding similar, but smaller off-diagonal submatrices whenever there are regional trade groups. However, in general it should be possible to consider world trade matrices in all 3-digit SITC (or other digit) commodities and attempt arrangement of the countries in the manner suggested to discover which are pure H.O. goods.

In the case of border-trade goods it is possible to reorder countries such that those with common borders adjoin each other and result in square submatrices along the diagonal. In Fig. 11.2, we show the actual OECD matrix of trade in Stone, sand and gravel (SITC 273) for 1967–8 ordered in this manner. As can be seen, we have been moderately successful in finding matrices containing 'large' elements while the rest of the elements are zero or small. Only the US–Canada matrix appears to be an unqualified success by this criterion and even in this case there remains a surprisingly high level of trade between Italy and the United States. This bilateral trade consists largely of Carrera marble and Vermont granite.

In the case of the remaining matrix elements outside the square submatrices our problem is due to the fact that countries typically border on more than one other country and that this fact cannot be reflected adequately in a two-dimensional array.

We might report briefly that we were unsuccessful in testing the hypothesis that bilateral trade in sand, stone and gravel is a function of the length of common borders. Apparently the hypothesis is too simple, given the differences in the cost of transport across bodies of water and land with many topographical characteristics and many forms of transport.

Cycle goods, such as seasonal agricultural products, should in principle show up as pure H.O. goods during the appropriate seasons of the year. Thus trade in fresh fruits among countries with temperate climates of the northern and southern hemispheres should permit arrangement of matrices as shown in Fig. 11.1, for any one growing season, and an analogous pattern with the rectangle of transpose elements on the opposite side of the diagonal.

Lastly, we have some speculative ideas on the configuration of a trade matrix representing the analytically pure case of differentiated manufactures. Figure 11.3 represents such a case. The horizontal axis lists countries in the order $1, \ldots n$, while in the vertical array the order is reversed, $n, \ldots 1$. Under this order the zero elements which show no international trade from one country to itself are on the diagonal from bottom left to top right. This triangularised matrix configuration is justified on the following grounds. Consider country 1 to be the United States, the largest national market in the world for a differentiated product such as cars. This large market is assumed to be of sufficient size that all n countries producing cars find it profitable to establish sales outlets in and export to it some of the styles and qualities of cars they produce. As a result, country 1 is shown to import cars from all n countries. At the same time, the domestic market in country 1 is large enough

Figure 11.2

International Trade in Stone, Sand and Gravel, 1967–8

From \ To	USA	Canada	Aus-tralia	Switzer-land	West Ger.	Belg.- Luxem.	Nether-lands	France	Italy	Nor-way	Sweden	Den-mark	UK	Japan
USA	—	125											1	2
Canada	105	—												
Austria			1	3	18	1	1	1	1	1	4	4	1	
Switzerland				—	12						4	2		4
West Germany		13		24	—	55	187	6	7	3	4		1	
Belgium–Luxembourg			1	3	28	—	100	76	27		5	2	8	1
Netherlands	4			19	8	82	—	16	8		2	2	1	
France	22	5	8	17	72	54	16	—	45	14	5	7	4	4
Italy	2	2		1	63	21	8	34	—	14	5	2	22	
Norway	1	1		1	24	4	14	14	11	—	2	7	7	1
Sweden		2		1	31	3	1	3	5	2	—	11	5	
Denmark	1				31	1	4	3		1	1	—		
UK		1			3	1	4	3		1	1	2	—	1
Japan														

Numbers have been rounded. The empty cells indicate the value of trade was less than $50,000.
Source: OECD, *Commodity Trade, Exports and Imports*, 1967.

to permit the production of styles and varieties having some appeal in all countries of the world. Consequently country 1 also is shown to export cars to every one of the n countries in the world.

Now let us assume country 2 to be somewhat smaller than 1 and country 3 smaller than 2, etc. down to the smallest country, n, and that the number of different product styles produced, consumed, exported and imported are related to this national market size. Under these assumptions we would obtain the kind of world trade matrix shown in Fig. 11.3. In it country n is shown to trade only with country 1.

Figure 11.3
Matrix of Trade in Differentiated Manufactures

Exports to Imports from	Country 1	2	3	4	.	.	$n-1$	n
Country n	×							—
$n-1$	×	×					—	
.	×	×	×				—	
.	×	×	×	×	—			
4	×	×	×	—	×			
3	×	×	—	×	×	×		
2	×	—	×	×	×	×	×	
1	—	×	×	×	×	×	×	×

We are fully aware of the fact that the preceding 'explanation' of world trade matrices in differentiated products is based on many strong assumptions which are likely not to be met in the real world. Furthermore, we have not even spelt out a host of assumptions about factor endowments, transport costs, protection, etc. which can readily be seen to influence trade even in the presence of strong economies of scale in the production of differentiated products, which are the main concern of this book. Any empirical study of trade matrices would have to modify the crude model we presented, by taking account of these factors.

DETERMINANTS OF COMMODITY COMPOSITION OF TRADE

Traditional empirical tests of the Heckscher–Ohlin model, like those by MacDougall (1951), Keesing (1966) and Balassa (1963),

have as their objective the documentation of functional relationships between country i's imports from country j of commodity
k, and independent variables like unit labour costs, capital–
labour ratios, ratios of skilled to unskilled labour, research
expenditure per unit of sales and others, reflecting the relative
scarcity of factors of production in each country. In principle,
analogous studies could be carried out to 'explain' trade in
differentiated products and test the models of Part II.

One immediate difficulty encountered in such studies is the
statistical quantification of differences in traded commodities
distinguished by style, design, quality, functional characteristics or a combination of all of these features. As an ideal, one
might attempt quantification of these goods characteristics as
has been suggested by Lancaster (1966) and carried out by
Griliches (1962) and others in their calculation of hedonic
price indices.

Let us assume that either by such econometric methods or
some, more casual methods it has been possible to establish the
characteristics of close-substitute products traded between two
countries, i and j. Then it should be possible to generate
independent variables serving as proxies for the theoretical
determinants of trade we developed in Part II. For example,
Linder's model suggests that countries with high *per capita*
incomes export high-quality products and import low-quality
products from countries with lower *per capita* incomes. Our
model emphasising other cultural and historic determinants of
tastes and production implies that countries with long average
distances between cities should produce and export large cars,
those with short distances produce small cars. Countries with
high population density produce small and light furniture,
countries with low density produce large and heavy furniture.
It seems that, generally, empirical studies of the determinants
of differentiated-product trade must be more *ad hoc* and in the
nature of case studies than the traditional model testing. This
style of research is demanded both by the nature of the problem
and the availability of data.

Our measure of intra-industry trade lends itself to the
formulation and testing of hypotheses about differences in the
measure among countries or industries. At the most general
level, one would expect intra-industry trade of countries to be

an increasing function of the size of their markets, which can be expected to be the product of population size and *per capita* income. Other determinants of inter-country differences are the levels of protection, distance from other countries, and the share of manufacturing industry in GNP.

Tests of intra-industry trade levels among industries should use as independent variables proxies representing the strength of product differentiation. Two such proxies, borrowed from industrial organisation studies, might be advertising expenditures per dollar of sales and industry concentration ratios.

The product-cycle hypothesis suggests that intra-industry trade across industries is an increasing function of research expenditures per dollar of sales, ratio of highly to unskilled labour, average age of products, etc. In some cases it may be useful to combine the relevant independent variables in one multiple regression.

In general, empirical work related to the explanation of international trade in differentiated products can be expected to be rather difficult because of the many, often non-quantified ways in which products are differentiated, the special considerations introduced by market organisation and the elusive nature of economies of scale due to the length of runs. Nevertheless it seems to us that the empirical study of trade in differentiated products, which represents such a large proportion of total world trade, as we have documented in Part I, is a promising undertaking.

Appendix

TABLE A3.1
Intra-Industry Trade, 1964

SITC Classes	Canada	US	Japan	Belgium–Luxembourg	Netherlands	Germany	France	Italy	UK	Australia	Mean†
001	62	78	52	73	91	52	79	03	71	54	62
011	94	73	17	66	31	12	54	01	07	01	36
012	89	51	*	92	56	86	48	15	01	00	55
013	96	93	53	91	20	20	70	90	09	04	55
022	11	32	35	86	33	39	46	08	66	00	36
023	00	16	00	40	19	02	30	00	00	00	11
024	88	18	00	27	11	38	64	82	04	31	36
025	72	17	40	07	01	01	27	06	27	00	20
031	15	10	78	54	46	57	35	04	38	93	43
032	42	46	02	05	99	32	14	11	10	04	27
041	*	01	00	60	33	17	43	03	00	00	17
042	00	01	00	37	50	17	12	09	*	07	13
043	*	33	00	23	99	06	00	00	41	08	23
044	02	01	00	09	06	10	69	15	*	*	14
045	02	08	00	02	32	15	93	14	03	00	17
046	*	*	87	12	11	12	07	05	07	*	18
047	29	*	18	10	57	00	00	100	11	00	28
048	72	73	30	54	54	54	66	93	40	16	55
051	24	76	20	43	59	01	26	15	01	30	30
052	01	22	02	10	05	03	12	47	00	05	11
053	19	70	72	39	91	09	71	14	13	07	41
054	53	88	16	88	20	13	46	57	10	83	47
055	51	97	61	87	78	07	96	15	18	46	56

061	27	02	37	00	79	25	16	87	02	05	17
062	61	100	19	74	49	54	41	91	70	93	17
071	07	07	13	01	02	03	22	06	01	06	06
072	20	00	12	50	09	10	99	07	05	02	10
073	56	50	95	34	99	44	38	68	40	42	49
074	19	07	00	00	00	05	23	53	82	04	19
075	31	00	22	37	22	18	98	13	74	14	11
081	42	53	11	28	68	29	69	41	19	51	53
091	31	00	15	57	16	68	47	90	18	00	00
099	64	21	69	91	52	82	32	98	87	32	72
0‡	25	07	15	18	44	16	40	49	15	25	18
111	28	00	11	17	10	85	54	62	00	43	00
112	58	77	71	33	96	54	90	44	68	05	46
121	20	02	00	54	13	02	21	14	28	42	25
122	35	44	28	10	66	24	74	77	03	08	20
1	42	37	44	37	88	25	56	43	30	24	40
211	50	05	34	32	40	51	88	77	02	94	78
212	36	56	04	02	78	08	53	29	00	49	78
221	18	13	01	02	23	01	13	18	00	15	97
231	42	04	32	45	46	33	74	15	10	92	69
241	31	00	11	05	13	32	52	41	00	93	67
242	26	04	04	01	50	12	25	56	01	47	62
243	29	48	00	02	63	15	04	23	67	48	15
244	14	00	00	83	31	00	00	00	00	*	*
251	17	00	03	02	22	14	30	20	00	74	06
261	09	03	06	34	11	18	00	00	20	03	00
262	31	00	61	08	76	20	45	61	13	06	16
263	07	00	05	02	04	18	18	12	02	08	04

Table A3.1 (*continued*)

SITC Classes	Canada	US	Japan	Belgium–Luxembourg	Netherlands	Germany	France	Italy	UK	Australia	Mean†
264	45	00	03	32	38	07	03	03	04	00	14
265	01	02	01	91	91	04	78	28	02	00	30
266	72	89	03	63	51	33	69	49	80	12	52
267	55	41	60	68	54	85	82	17	62	20	54
271	11	11	00	15	04	14	10	01	00	00	07
273	86	78	29	89	54	75	99	57	31	67	67
274	29	78	00	10	03	07	60	16	02	00	21
275	42	51	18	95	100	44	45	92	33	28	55
276	20	54	04	53	78	54	73	36	87	41	50
281	32	32	00	04	16	02	66	18	00	62	23
282	86	07	00	36	25	78	60	01	04	02	30
283	48	34	00	05	08	08	09	45	03	06	17
284	21	46	01	57	66	45	46	39	52	15	39
285	*	*	00	50	08	00	09	00	03	00	09
286	*	67	*	00	*	00	05	00	00	00	09
291	94	75	25	91	80	40	71	57	16	67	62
292	78	74	51	84	24	27	58	77	15	43	53
2	33	42	05	49	35	23	47	18	22	05	28
321	25	07	01	44	82	36	08	03	03	07	22
331	90	01	00	00	00	00	00	00	01	01	09
332	20	73	16	82	55	73	73	33	72	68	56
341	07	30	06	37	61	23	89	42	25	00	32
351	81	*	*	*	86	*	70	*	72	00	62
3	63	31	03	43	42	31	21	09	28	22	29

411	36	19	14	24	63	50	24	39	84	09	37
421	47	00	16	53	56	30	87	84	70	23	47
422	30	10	12	00	19	18	93	43	53	24	31
431	47	59	75	36	37	64	44	99	21	23	10
4	39	17	19	34	35	35	64	57	76	17	35
512	72	21	93	88	97	62	95	69	88	46	66
513	79	20	99	71	81	60	97	100	84	86	92
514	67	19	69	91	51	64	55	91	69	65	96
515	24	00	18	29	21	36	86	00	00	06	43
521	52	00	63	05	77	92	77	64	48	20	76
531	43	47	59	34	83	26	56	37	57	80	00
532	53	71	85	73	80	59	60	77	00	48	00
533	57	37	27	62	88	42	70	95	86	16	11
541	53	45	22	99	62	42	65	65	68	25	43
551	50	23	83	52	76	50	66	32	12	75	13
553	52	58	39	62	10	89	67	63	42	71	50
554	52	04	26	39	79	39	83	74	98	12	17
561	50	47	48	18	83	18	65	60	86	84	32
571	49	71	10	48	52	38	21	85	14	73	100
581	61	37	85	69	98	49	98	67	66	15	43
599	56	66	76	55	70	63	73	67	40	14	37
5	60	29	68	68	78	51	81	67	72	38	51
611	69	63	98	87	52	81	99	13	33	88	75
612	63	37	68	20	93	75	77	84	18	93	65
613	74	*	99	30	94	86	33	76	100	66	85
621	56	14	57	89	98	51	69	44	42	*	36
629	53	26	33	52	41	99	99	91	08	40	46
631	37	25	08	22	48	92	36	75	02	16	49

Table A3.1 (*continued*)

SITC Classes	Canada	US	Japan	Belgium–Luxembourg	Netherlands	Germany	France	Italy	UK	Australia	Mean†
632	33	75	05	71	56	83	97	52	33	46	55
633	00	68	67	25	88	09	26	56	59	00	40
641	12	54	57	72	87	46	69	55	39	15	51
642	47	35	20	88	87	72	58	86	46	41	58
651	28	52	08	67	94	71	43	24	55	23	46
652	25	90	03	62	75	87	43	97	67	04	55
653	14	58	15	72	94	91	65	34	60	11	51
654	13	83	19	67	43	66	22	87	85	04	49
655	60	66	09	78	100	62	90	95	38	22	62
656	14	48	09	44	80	84	63	74	89	10	51
657	37	29	14	26	97	37	74	77	93	05	49
661	96	47	07	22	07	93	67	24	88	75	53
662	41	95	06	97	95	69	80	89	59	09	64
663	18	26	68	76	81	86	80	89	44	38	61
664	05	91	37	20	68	61	43	37	58	14	43
665	02	67	34	60	28	59	58	75	87	11	48
666	00	06	01	52	65	30	90	86	30	00	36
667	17	28	70	97	97	70	65	19	*	89	61
671	49	53	06	46	78	83	67	15	22	70	49
672	09	68	04	69	63	94	76	15	54	20	47
673	33	47	02	19	26	77	85	89	57	50	48
674	75	85	01	22	83	94	66	76	49	94	64
675	*	68	18	14	42	74	91	54	78	15	50
676	13	20	14	15	21	10	31	81	00	18	22
677	03	46	04	09	50	49	76	74	17	87	41

678	34	100	03	67	42	32	53	44	24	74	47
679	66	18	00	16	39	58	59	84	21	00	36
681	83	39	03	81	38	68	27	18	95	18	47
682	14	74	42	93	37	56	29	41	46	86	52
683	20	32	13	11	27	41	55	13	96	08	32
684	23	86	95	89	63	73	68	87	40	100	72
685	03	15	04	46	41	46	56	02	36	00	25
686	02	60	20	29	96	26	69	09	15	01	33
687	00	18	01	82	17	19	04	06	98	28	27
688	*	00	00	00	00	00	00	00	00	00	00
689	83	87	98	88	79	33	50	85	60	97	76
691	99	16	15	98	75	49	56	52	14	20	49
692	33	21	23	83	80	56	64	28	45	94	53
693	60	73	07	13	55	37	71	87	34	71	51
694	49	61	07	79	73	38	90	78	63	41	58
695	19	47	33	68	66	40	92	75	53	39	53
696	44	45	11	18	100	34	89	87	40	06	47
697	20	96	26	93	96	38	92	55	52	19	59
698	22	67	30	85	70	36	99	74	44	53	58

6	27	58	13	60	72	66	63	48	52	31	49
711	68	44	93	89	55	49	96	88	44	15	64
712	73	37	94	87	65	42	64	97	19	13	59
714	60	38	20	30	100	74	81	60	93	07	56
715	20	17	54	68	53	31	78	96	75	13	50
717	27	72	50	91	51	35	80	84	59	11	56
718	36	20	87	50	68	39	100	100	56	30	59
719	29	21	100	75	66	38	95	95	61	22	60
722	41	21	72	78	73	40	70	90	52	14	55
723	84	55	10	96	82	40	58	72	17	35	55

Appendix

Table A3.1 (*continued*)

SITC Classes	Canada	US	Japan	Belgium–Luxembourg	Netherlands	Germany	France	Italy	UK	Australia	Mean†
724	69	62	12	67	93	40	86	92	56	21	60
725	43	31	20	27	87	37	86	38	41	61	47
726	48	72	84	65	51	29	82	99	98	00	63
729	27	34	53	75	91	55	89	81	69	27	60
731	58	23	08	47	73	12	35	39	11	32	34
732	35	64	19	81	34	23	65	55	18	22	42
733	29	86	10	61	81	46	42	33	13	07	41
734	57	14	14	83	50	51	71	81	53	11	48
735	43	21	25	77	28	18	59	35	77	86	47
7	45	38	42	76	66	36	79	78	46	20	53
812	49	56	18	84	87	61	93	97	71	39	65
821	46	91	26	79	79	65	73	47	80	52	64
831	07	29	17	57	82	56	49	18	85	04	40
841	33	36	06	76	58	73	59	15	76	25	46
842	07	48	00	63	43	97	06	50	37	50	40
851	36	13	03	70	70	52	48	02	75	16	38
861	64	56	38	37	73	43	88	84	84	24	59
862	26	60	66	18	73	67	94	94	67	38	60
863	11	32	94	52	44	46	74	68	64	19	50
864	20	26	87	10	23	54	96	46	59	07	43
891	09	80	22	93	91	38	95	89	91	13	62
892	17	50	82	100	67	52	93	50	62	25	60
893	13	95	18	94	69	57	91	56	90	35	62
894	38	61	21	92	56	76	91	66	92	45	64

37	27	47	30	68	21	96	70	68	23	49
89	26	21	95	98	72	30	79	97	39	65
30	86	36	57	41	55	73	11	59	17	46
06	42	25	75	69	59	87	48	93	16	52
39	49	25	69	71	57	75	37	79	26	53
*	*	*	43	*	00	*	*	16	00	15
24	78	41	27	57	44	*	*	*	92	52
93	*	*	77	*	*	12	25	45	100	59
90	06	00	00	*	63	55	78	58	00	39
*	*	*	80	*	48	*	00	51	00	36
29	62	41	28	57	44	02	67	30	90	45
35	40	21	60	58	42	60	44	40	17	42
37	48	23	62	64	44	63	49	46	17	45

Row labels (top to bottom): 895, 896, 897, 899, 8, 911, 931, 941, 951, 961, 9, All Commodities Unadjusted average, Adjusted average

Source: First nine countries: OECD Foreign Trade Statistics, *Commodity Trade Statistics, Commodity Trade Imports* and *Exports, January–December 1964.* Australia: *Commodity Trade Statistics 1964,* UN Statistical Papers, Series D, vol. XIV.

* Indicates either export or import not available. In the aggregation these 3-digit elements are treated as zeros.

† The industry averages in the extreme right column are the unweighted means of individual countries' statistics.

‡ The 1-digit statistics of each country are the averages of the 3-digit elements, using the sums of export and import trade as weights.

Appendix

TABLE A3.2
Intra-Industry Trade, 1959

SITC Classes 1963 (Revised 1959)	Canada	US	Japan	Belgium–Luxembourg	Netherlands	Germany	France	Italy	UK	Australia	Mean
001	33	43	80	38	53	02	37	01	40	00	33
011	66	42	70	89	30	19	89	01	02	01	41
012	74	69	50	34	19	37	86	44	02	00	41
013	82	32	75	100	18	38	27	89	09	10	48
022	01	01	20	62	06	04	44	00	64	00	20
023	00	08	00	02	01	00	72	00	01	00	08
024	91	31	00	03	02	24	69	95	03	18	34
025	48	04	08	25	01	01	43	01	03	00	13
031	12	04	01	40	36	56	71	03	54	99	38
032	43	42	01	08	85	40	27	09	07	06	27
041	00	04	01	41	03	03	90	20	*	00	18
042	*	01	01	67	69	09	42	01	*	00	21
043		25	01	00	35	01	74	00	44	00	20
044	11	01	02	03	01	01	32	01	*	00	06
045	00	08	29	03	12	42	33	15	15	00	13
046	00	01	23	92	03	09	78	01	04	00	22
047	80	74	79	22	78	86	62	18	22	00	39
048	74	82	77	74	24	62	36	72	59	11	56
051	16	25	01	32	89	01	19	12	01	26	35
052	07	67	47	06	03	03	53	47	*	04	17
053	09	61	71	34	87	05	78	08	10	08	35
054	35	80	49	88	16	21	45	22	10	77	45
055	43	09	04	79	50	07	65	22	31	47	47
061	16	90	50	69	71	71	00	79	41	06	37
062	05	03	00	56	16	42	20	43	22	86	43
071	01			14	17	05	03	00	25	08	08

Code											
072	20	01	23	60	06	07	96	04	01	02	00
073	44	58	85	53	21	45	30	92	16	38	03
074	14	06	*	01	08	15	19	25	61	01	08
075	26	04	16	10	23	13	82	14	85	09	02
081	49	13	05	66	55	36	59	40	92	65	62
091	24	00	19	01	02	31	02	91	06	02	87
099	46	35	26	52	20	63	56	78	13	40	74
0	22	06	12	19	49	13	31	40	12	21	18
111	23	40	09	18	10	40	80	24	00	05	01
112	53	78	70	24	81	70	47	15	98	04	43
121	27	01	01	85	35	01	13	09	54	49	23
122	45	47	14	47	62	40	66	75	47	12	36
1	40	25	37	43	76	31	35	24	62	31	39
211	48	04	24	35	42	38	88	76	04	84	85
212	42	54	02	11	96	12	67	32	00	52	92
221	15	03	01	03	08	01	12	10	00	38	75
231	17	00	10	36	04	14	12	31	00	62	04
241	38	00	25	04	08	30	29	100	100	55	29
242	31	08	07	01	63	11	31	61	02	84	47
243	30	73	01	01	91	12	04	16	44	41 *	22 *
244	16	00	*	77	30	04	04	00	08	49	08 *
251	17	00	03	06	15	26	38	18	08	02	20
261	09	02	00	69	01	00	00	00	05	17	01 *
262	33	00	59	09	77	21	46	74	06	13	00 *
263	06	00	05	03	05	10	12	14	01	00	80
264	04	00	*	03	02	13	07	11	00	01	08
265	31	00	06	61	54	07	100	78	00	99	
266	47	12	57	43	66	31	71	83	23	58	
267	60	00	50	09	99	87	62	58	88	83	
271	16	00	02	01	36	14	07	04	03		

Table A3.2 (*continued*)

SITC Classes 1963 (Revised 1959)	Canada	US	Japan	Belgium–Luxembourg	Netherlands	Germany	France	Italy	UK	Australia	Mean
273 274 275 276 } 272	46	57	05	52	62	56	71	89	63	49	55
281	30	20	00	07	17	03	27	32	01	00	14
282	74	13	00	82	44	79	36	01	02	00	33
283	19	17	01	09	09	04	10	78	05	05	16
284	37	44	04	61	63	25	89	18	45	03	39
285	*	*	*	00	00	00	*	00	*	00	00
286 } 283.19	*	*	*	*	*	*	*	*	*	*	00
291	99	80	55	91	85	33	70	74	12	78	68
292	88	57	79	98	28	29	68	82	14	51	59
2	29	39	04	45	33	20	42	21	21	05	26
321 } 311	11	02	03	50	81	47	27	02	12	03	24
331 } 312	43	02	00	01	00	00	01	04	01	00	05
332 } 313	11	87	25	84	63	73	58	22	77	69	57
341 } 314	42	67	00	*	00	73	57	*	*	00	34
351 } 315	16	*	00	*	94	*	78	*	*	00	38
3	30	40	05	49	48	40	22	09	33	26	30
411	47	10	91	57	14	45	74	05	14	06	36
421 422 } 412	25	60	98	51	97	18	35	26	26	03	44
431 } 413	30	44	34	84	38	56	47	05	86	62	49
4	31	44	92	57	62	29	40	19	28	10	41

512	60	16	98	79	97	56	93	67	31	31	31
511	68	19	68	92	59	48	69	79	72	88	87
513 514 515											
521	51	00	08	32	87	88	93	84	13	84	19
531	41	00	48	56	87	21	53	00	28	74	*
532	42	23	55	61	68	85	61	40	00	29	*
533	46	83	12	34	78	27	55	57	74	19	24
541	53	28	19	90	40	42	76	66	96	26	48
551	46	28	78	39	79	47	68	25	16	78	04
552	42	90	07	40	15	48	82	91	14	21	08
561	44	48	35	27	38	11	41	48	56	94	39
591	40	69	01	93	35	36	21	62	00	40	*
553 554											
571 581 599											
599	62	30	70	81	87	55	83	62	50	16	86
5	56	27	56	69	65	46	74	61	51	43	68
611	69	20	91	66	37	92	87	86	49	72	93
612	55	67	54	24	93	53	93	75	00	79	09
613	55	00	92	44	94	99	30	55	00	70	70
621	47	00	57	98	84	22	44	80	69	00	13
629	49	46	11	53	23	67	81	88	07	53	60
631	41	46	02	29	36	99	47	84	01	19	51
632	52	59	39	41	35	77	64	53	03	98	55
633	38	00	42	67	25	20	93	00	00	99	*
641	49	07	53	61	96	46	91	71	17	40	11
642	45	43	31	100	27	47	76	54	13	43	17
651	39	09	33	17	15	68	99	49	10	55	33
652	42	02	93	39	11	74	65	70	01	60	07
653	42	04	41	20	23	89	99	72	06	58	04
654	46	00	96	69	05	67	30	62	02	82	*
655	53	25	22	73	34	72	92	84	07	80	45
656	46	06	72	19	44	95	97	60	04	52	10

Table A3.2 (*continued*)

SITC Classes 1963 (Revised 1959)	Canada	US	Japan	Belgium–Luxembourg	Netherlands	Germany	France	Italy	UK	Australia	Mean
657	01	33	02	20	50	53	62	42	76	02	34
661	99	64	03	23	25	86	32	32	24	88	48
662	38	91	22	81	91	76	96	93	29	11	63
663	29	19	40	62	28	38	91	93	27	20	45
664	12	72	19	11	73	41	16	24	40	07	31
665	04	66	14	65	48	34	33	95	87	09	45
666	13	10	00	35	81	17	41	81	23	03	30
672	23	06	24	99	95	94	88	94	*	75	66
667 } 671 672 673 674 675 676 677 678 679 681 681			32							85	59
682	09	64	94	96	40	73	37	27	65	51	56
683	06	26	23	60	20	46	60	11	95	00	35
684	08	62	85	87	74	85	67	95	51	03	62
685	05	05	40	46	38	73	52	06	21	00	29
686	06 *	31	100	02	88	43	68	64	12	05	42
687		04	00 *	52	78	66	04	03	05	19 *	26
688	00	00		00	00	00	00	00	00		00
689	70	56	81	69	98	52	69	61	08	61	62
691	10	11	23	29	85	23	42	33	20	00	28

	50	53	24	65	51	19	91	79	15	87	18
692 693 694 695 696 697 698 } 699											
681.01	40	*	86	03	92	96	00	30	*	05	10
681.02	44	*	29	68	32	68	08	32	*	25	90
681.03	59	*	76	52	90	83	45	40	*	44	45
681.04	37	*	18	93	33	69	10	06	*	39	31
681.05	66	*	69	91	44	85	90	14	*	47	88
681.06	58	*	29	70	83	68	52	15	*	88	*
681.07	39	*	01	81	27	81	73	11	*	34	05
681.08	23	*	00	18	18	18	20	05	*	18	90
681.11	24	*	00	15	11	10	53	05	*	24	71
681.12	47	*	27	84	22	67	66	34	*	32	40
681.13	39	*	07	21	19	17	54	48	*	94	48
681.14	52	*	14	80	23	47	80	58	*	68	42
6	43	27	44	47	39	63	74	53	14	50	21
711	54	12	43	78	96	47	73	75	41	13	62
712	62	39	51	37	61	23	73	84	64	90	95
714	57	05	86	47	96	64	99	54	22	48	53
715	41	09	67	74	62	27	46	81	10	20	19
716	56	17	41	99	99	33	73	75	85	17	19
717 718 719 722 } 721		16							32		
723 724 725 } 721.01	24	*	14	82	50	25	56	94	*	26	21
726 729 } 721.12	46	*	40	89	46	37	66	28	*	03	07
	40										

Table A3.2 (*continued*)

SITC Classes 1963 (Revised 1959)	Canada	US	Japan	Belgium–Luxembourg	Netherlands	Germany	France	Italy	UK	Australia	Mean
731	33	01	16	32	40	10	23	31	07	27	22
732	18	94	36	61	29	19	12	19	13	13	31
733	11	90	06	96	97	25	22	16	08	15	39
734	57	17	17	53	98	42	78	95	17	17	49
735	58	09	15	47	45	16	75	16	45	22	35
7	34	43	36	66	61	28	58	60	31	15	43
812	10	17	06	72	91	40	47	81	40	14	42
821	12	71	13	43	84	58	35	45	60	78	50
831	04	52	00	30	93	23	19	29	80	00	33
841	13	51	01	91	80	99	14	13	95	11	47
842	88	93	*	100	80	80	00	00	70	00	57
851	28	25	00	72	87	61	22	02	99	64	46
861	25	52	48	34	76	24	78	63	76	18	49
862	39	67	48	13	40	59	47	89	46	53	50
863	20	31	64	09	45	95	88	70	*	30	50
864	19	17	95	06	23	44	54	08	65	04	33
891	12	83	45	78	98	28	43	67	63	11	53
892	12	48	80	95	59	55	72	64	48	26	56
899	14	96	02	47	35	20	19	25	43	10	31
893, 894, 895, 899, 897 } 873	22	42	04	53	74	79	32	44	78	33	46
8	18	47	13	61	79	60	40	33	74	25	45

	911	921	931	951} 961	963	9	Unadjusted average	Adjusted average
	20	34	00	28	00	34		36
	*	52	00	00	00	46		14
	18	00	*	20	*	18	32	35
	00	00	*	33	*	33	35	38
	00	53	*	23	*	04	45	47
	00	*	*	42	*	52	39	42
	61	48	*	85	*	62	55	58
	58	02	*	29	*	23	53	54
	*	*	00	23	00	12	17	17
	00	72	*	11	*	54	40	43
	20	43	*	10	*	37	28	29

Source: All countries except Japan and Australia: OEEC, *Foreign Trade by Commodities January–December 1959.*
Japan and Australia: *Commodity Trade Statistics January–December 1959,* UN Statistical Papers, Series D, vol. IX.

Notes

1 The trade data used in compiling this table were classified according to the original 1950 SITC rather than the 1963 (revised) SITC which was used for both 1964 and 1967 data. These classifications differ for some 3-digit classes but the differences were reduced by using the 5-digit subdivisions of some of the 3-digit classes for 1959 to obtain classes roughly comparable to the classes of the 1963 (rev.) SITC. This was done for the 1959 Classes 681, Iron and Steel, and 721, Electric machinery, apparatus and appliances. The twelve 5-digit subdivisions of Iron and steel correspond quite closely to the ten 3-digit classes of the 1963 (rev.) SITC Division 67, Iron and steel. The remaining differences between the two classifications are not serious. Where the classifications differ, the 1963 (rev.) 3-digit classes which correspond to the 1950 classes employed in the table have also been given in the extreme left column.

2 For both Japan and Australia in 1959 the 5-digit statistics were not available for classes 681 and 721, and the 3-digit trade data were used instead. This results in a slight overstatement of the average intra-industry trade for these two countries.

3 Some 5-digit components have been included in the wrong 3-digit classes, as indicated in the 'Commodity notes' to the OEEC statistics. However, the misclassifications are generally quite minor.

TABLE A3.3
Yugoslavian Intra-Industry Trade

Industry*	1961	1964	1968	Industry	1961	1964	1968
00	34	43	7	56	19	12	40
01	6	2	7	59	50	54	67
02	85	70	38	Average 5	43	40	50
03	51	73	60				
04	48	6	80	61	24	48	85
05	53	49	92	62	7	25	18
06	39	36	41	63	6	55	50
07	7	16	6	64	43	94	87
08	36	18	46	65	54	81	71
09	100	33	41	66	97	97	85
Average 0	46	35	42	67	32	45	56
				68	86	75	77
11	17	6	34	69	85	96	75
12	2	11	4	Average 6	48	68	67
Average 1	9	8	19				
				71	24	31	30
21	9	3	25	72	70	72	85
22	68	51	91	73	66	98	83
23	0	0	2	Average 7	53	67	66
24	8	8	28				
25	82	99	92	81	94	89	99
26	25	14	17	82	1	4	9
27	93	77	65	83	6	4	52
28	81	98	96	84	55	29	41
29	56	53	66	85	11	2	21
Average 2	53	50	60	86	12	10	17
				89	80	68	58
Total 3	29	31	3	Average 8	37	30	42
Total 4	3	6	21	Total 9	89	13	36
51	74	66	66	Average			
52	55	8	16	0–9	41	35	41
53	39	35	38				
54	24	39	85				
55	38	64	41				

* For description of SITC industry classes see Table 3.1 in the text.
Source: Vukasovich (1970).

Intra-Industry Trade in South-East Asia, 1962 (%)

2-Digit Groups	Ceylon	India	Korea	Malaya	Pakistan	Philippines	Taiwan	Thailand
51	21	7	0	0	1	0	24	1
52	0	77	—	—	0	—	—	—
53	0	5	0	0	2	0	0	0
54	0	16	0	25	4	0	0	1
55	74	37	—	58	8	0	0	3
56	0	0	0	0	0	0	18	0
57	0	0	0	0	0	0	0	0
58	0	1	0	0	0	0	97	0
59	0	10	0	0	2	0	0	4
61	82	1	—	45	24	—	0	94
62	0	52	0	—	7	0	0	7
63	2	31	0	0	1	0	78	100
64	0	11	0	22	42	20	12	1
65	1	13	14	27	30	0	0	3
66	17	44	4	8	10	0	6	79
67	0	5	5	5	0	0	78	1
68	0	0	6	0	1	0	0	0
69	0	27	22	0	3	0	0	3
71	0	2	2	15	2	0	0	0
72	0	4	1	0	2	0	0	1
73	0	2	27	24	4	0	0	0
81	0	50	0	0	2	0	63	1
82	12	50	78	17	2	67	71	9
83	0	6	7	0	39	100	43	3
84	0	5	0	0	38	0	0	27
85	0	0	0	0	10	—	0	7
86	0	21	0	0	21	0	0	0
89								
Average	4	8	5	12	9	2	15	4

Source: Hesketh (1973).

TABLE A9.1

Share of Intra-Industry Trade in Total Trade Among ECC Countries, 1967

SITC Classes	Belgium–Luxembourg	Netherlands	Germany	France	Italy	Mean
00 Live animals	48	17	48	94	1	42
01 Meat and meat preparations	33	13	20	96	10	34
02 Dairy products and eggs	84	35	61	36	19	47
03 Fish and fish preparations	58	23	81	39	25	45
04 Cereals and cereal preparations	67	78	10	18	74	49
05 Fruit and vegetables	99	40	8	98	12	51
06 Sugar, sugar preparations and honey	71	85	28	35	77	59
07 Coffee, tea, cocoa, spices	69	42	50	48	59	54
08 Feeding stuff for animals	91	78	76	62	29	67
09 Miscellaneous food preparations	52	57	88	40	81	64
0	70	38	27	59	54	50
11 Beverages	64	91	28	29	69	56
12 Tobacco and tobacco manufactures	86	78	65	26	61	63
1	74	82	38	29	66	58
21 Hides, skins and fur skins, undressed	93	90	77	51	19	66
22 Oil-seeds, oil nuts and oil kernels	58	99	56	34	6	51
23 Crude rubber (incl. synthetic)	32	41	86	93	42	59
24 Wood, lumber and cork	86	49	87	20	7	37
25 Pulp and paper	30	80	71	88	5	55
26 Textile fibres (not manufactured into yarn or thread)	91	78	75	61	43	70
27 Crude fertilisers and minerals (excl. coal, petroleum)	98	75	100	80	86	88

28	Metalliferous ores and metal scrap	79	44	95	33	4	51
29	Crude animal and vegetable materials, n.e.s.	79	27	24	76	83	58
2		83	56	76	55	31	60
32	Coal, coke and briquettes	29	97	13	13	4	31
33	Petroleum and petroleum products	93	88	40	71	14	46
34	Gas, natural and manufactured	12	26	0	40	58	27
35	Electric energy	0	27	0	56	0	17
3		19	86	25	41	12	37
41	Animal oils and fats	78	79	63	86	35	68
42	Fixed vegetable oils and fats	98	49	9	92	15	53
43	Animal and vegetable oils and fats, processed	91	42	69	22	41	53
4		92	52	75	65	25	62
51	Chemical elements and compounds	82	93	72	92	72	82
52	Crude chemicals from coal, petroleum and gas	86	82	98	52	15	67
53	Dyeing, tanning and colouring materials	68	93	36	62	16	55
54	Medicinal and pharmaceutical products	60	94	70	90	58	74
55	Perfume materials, toilet and cleansing preparations	97	99	99	80	62	87
56	Fertilisers, manufactured	80	83	52	57	47	64
57	Explosives and pyrotechnic products	79	21	98	67	100	73
58	Plastic materials, etc.	89	85	78	65	94	82
59	Chemical materials and products, n.e.s.	70	93	64	88	38	71
5		80	91	70	79	67	77
61	Leather, leather manufactures, and dressed fur skins	81	97	66	54	80	76
62	Rubber manufactures, n.e.s.	79	96	91	75	92	87
63	Wood and cork manufactures (excl. furniture)	92	73	82	94	17	72

Table A9.1 (*continued*)

SITC Classes	Belgium–Luxembourg	Netherlands	Germany	France	Italy	Mean
64 Paper, paperboard and manufactures thereof	99	76	94	84	94	89
65 Textile yarn, fabrics, made-up articles, etc.	71	89	75	93	70	80
66 Non-metallic mineral manufactures, n.e.s.	66	61	86	73	89	75
67 Iron and steel	47	59	86	78	48	64
68 Non-ferrous metals	45	85	90	84	33	67
69 Manufactures of metal, n.e.s.	90	61	48	66	88	71
6	63	75	80	80	65	73
71 Machinery, other than electric	63	59	47	67	90	65
72 Electric machinery, apparatus and appliances	85	81	60	76	95	79
73 Transport equipment	100	48	77	97	81	81
7	84	64	59	78	89	75
81 Sanitary, plumbing, heating and lighting fixtures	93	66	46	45	74	65
82 Furniture	69	66	61	32	38	53
83 Travel goods, handbags and similar articles	66	67	100	97	22	70
84 Clothing	85	53	69	96	18	64
85 Footwear	50	65	27	97	2	48
86 Scientific instruments, photographic goods, watches, clocks	92	83	66	79	71	78
89 Miscellaneous manufactured articles, n.e.s.	93	75	75	71	50	73
8	85	66	65	76	35	65
91 Postal packages, not classified	23	0	0	0	0	5
93 Special transactions, not classified	14	72	100	0	0	37

94	Animals, n.e.s. – incl. zoo animals, dogs and cats	86	0	33	29	67	43
95	Firearms of war and ammunition	0	0	43	0	89	26
96	Coin – other than gold – not being legal tender	0	0	0	0	0	0
9		15	72	99	2	88	55
	All commodities						
	Unadjusted average	73	66	62	72	62	67
	Adjusted average	80	71	67	77	62	71

TABLE A9.2
Share of Intra-Industry Trade in Total Trade
Among EEC Countries, 1964

SITC Classes	Belgium–Luxembourg	Netherlands	Germany	France	Italy	Mean
00	54	13	32	8	7	23
01	81	8	19	77	18	41
02	95	11	24	53	36	44
03	48	31	86	42	21	46
04	85	68	7	21	74	51
05	89	32	4	82	10	43
06	85	96	31	21	17	50
07	71	43	30	80	45	54
08	91	55	52	52	27	55
09	78	45	67	58	68	63
0	82	28	17	58	22	41
11	60	71	23	23	52	46
12	92	66	97	62	93	82
1	74	68	37	25	67	54
21	98	86	94	62	50	78
22	69	70	22	42	16	44
23	35	38	80	98	79	66
24	92	65	64	13	8	48
25	100	75	79	75	12	68
26	89	83	89	51	35	69
27	96	69	91	77	99	86
28	35	48	74	26	15	40
29	86	23	22	78	67	55
2	84	58	70	48	40	60
32	47	92	12	9	2	32
33	88	60	46	55	29	56
34	35	74	28	68	57	52
35	0	86	0	90	0	35
3	61	75	22	25	21	41
41	73	91	85	93	78	84
42	100	39	42	91	75	69
43	94	59	65	29	48	59
4	92	56	62	73	66	70
51	78	77	67	91	76	78
52	82	96	92	66	0	67
53	71	99	39	60	19	58

SITC Classes	Belgium–Luxembourg	Netherlands	Germany	France	Italy	Mean
54	53	71	74	97	55	70
55	98	81	99	80	73	86
56	95	67	75	60	90	77
57	76	18	83	83	70	66
58	62	84	66	82	92	77
59	54	88	72	75	35	65
5	75	81	63	81	68	74
61	95	95	59	43	73	73
62	78	94	93	85	86	87
63	94	95	92	81	26	78
64	99	78	94	96	68	87
65	68	80	59	74	56	67
66	64	62	83	85	79	75
67	41	51	96	88	43	64
68	47	87	65	83	74	71
69	63	67	46	64	82	64
6	60	72	76	81	60	70
71	74	99	43	67	80	73
72	86	79	53	91	85	79
73	91	88	57	96	81	83
7	84	86	50	81	81	76
81	87	80	55	61	84	73
82	73	80	55	32	74	63
83	55	88	93	99	28	73
84	79	55	66	99	17	63
85	67	63	26	87	2	49
86	81	70	43	83	69	69
89	92	75	74	78	55	75
8	82	68	58	80	38	65
9	41	36	54	7	76	43
All commodities Unadjusted average	72	68	55	70	57	65
Adjusted average	76	70	59	73	58	68

TABLE A9.3

Share of Intra-Industry Trade in Total Trade Among EEC Countries, 1959

SITC Classes	Belgium–Luxembourg	Netherlands	Germany	France	Italy	Mean
00 Live animals	11	19	8	17	1	11
01 Meat and meat preparations	97	15	32	99	16	52
02 Dairy products, eggs and honey	55	3	10	52	33	31
03 Fish and fish preparations	35	17	99	64	12	45
04 Cereal and cereal preparations	94	96	52	30	40	62
05 Fruits and vegetables	70	25	6	68	8	35
06 Sugar and sugar preparations	93	47	49	60	10	52
07 Coffee, tea, cocoa, spices	44	38	37	30	90	48
08 Feeding stuff for animals	76	61	66	98	75	75
09 Miscellaneous food preparations	76	52	40	22	32	44
0	69	25	21	64	13	38
11 Beverages	19	84	32	18	46	40
12 Tobacco and tobacco manufactures	95	81	38	38	0	50
1	51	85	33	20	30	44
21 Hides, skins and fur skins, undressed	96	96	79	51	69	78
22 Oil-seeds, oil nuts and oil kernels	80	31	32	67	58	54
23 Crude rubber, including synthetic	81	35	93	75	58	68
24 Wood, lumber and cork	93	69	58	11	5	47
25 Pulp and waste paper	21	45	18	9	3	19
26 Textile fibres (not manufactured into yarn or thread)	94	86	67	39	31	63
27 Crude fertilisers and minerals, excl. coal, petroleum	70	59	95	79	89	78

Code							
28	Metalliferous ores and metal scrap	44	46	77	19	4	38
29	Animal and vegetable crude materials, n.e.s.	98	22	19	88	70	59
2		74	58	57	34	27	50
32	Coal, coke and briquettes*	47	99	20	24	0	38
33	Petroleum, crude and petroleum products*	93	64	47	84	24	62
34	Gas, natural and manufactured*	0	0	92	79	0	34
35	Electric energy*	0	86	0	50	0	27
3		64	81	26	33	12	43
41	Animal oils and fats*	84	83	83	40	0	58
42	Fixed vegetable oils*	79	22	82	34	45	52
43	Animal/vegetable oils and fats*	95	90	24	40	0	50
4		84	50	50	38	18	48
51	Chemical elements and compounds	79	91	41	82	51	69
52	Tar and crude chemicals from coal, petroleum and gas	90	99	93	84	64	86
53	Dyeing, tanning and colouring materials	27	92	30	61	32	48
54	Medicinal and pharmaceutical products	54	75	57	96	44	65
55	Perfume materials, toilet, cleansing preparations	85	83	93	71	85	83
56	Fertilisers, manufactured	84	0	64	68	8	45
57	Explosive and pyrotechnic products*	95	18	75	76	94	72
58	} Chemical materials and products n.e.s.*						
59	Chemical materials and products n.e.s.	51	99	55	100	57	72
5		70	85	51	83	53	68
61	Leather, leather manufactures and dressed furs	85	92	67	26	78	70
62	Rubber manufactures, n.e.s.	67	91	70	93	100	84
63	Wood and cork manufactures (excl. furniture)	90	81	85	51	47	71

Table A9.3 (*continued*)

SITC Classes	Belgium–Luxembourg	Netherlands	Germany	France	Italy	Mean
64 Paper, paperboard and manufactures thereof	86	78	85	66	55	74
65 Textile yarn, fabrics, made-up articles	74	78	43	32	35	52
66 Non-metallic mineral manufactures, n.e.s.	59	49	75	99	35	63
67 Silver, platinum, gems, jewellery	35	56	82	87	40	60
68 Base metals	87	55	29	69	84	65
69 Manufactures of metals	56	65	68	76	45	62
6						
71 Machinery other than electric	68	59	38	57	71	59
72 Electric machinery, apparatus and appliances	76	42	38	91	34	56
73 Transport equipment	64	36	77	49	42	54
7	67	48	51	55	60	56
81 Prefab. buildings; plumbing, heating and lighting fixtures	67	90	49	91	30	65
82 Furniture and fixtures	36	82	38	62	88	61
83 Travel goods, handbags and similar articles	14	85	63	92	67	64
84 Clothing	92	73	55	63	18	60
85 Footwear	54	94	30	77	2	51
86 Photographic equipment, watches, clocks	99	76	45	98	37	71
89 Musical instruments; manufactures, n.e.s.	66	78	90	93	75	80
8	75	78	66	87	39	69
91 Postal packages not classified*	53	37	0	0	0	18
93 Special transactions not classified*	0	0	52	0	0	10

94 Animals, n.e.s., including zoo animals, dogs and cats*	0	0	0	0	0	0
95 Firearms of war and ammunition*	29	29	45	93	11	41
96 Coin – other than gold – not being legal tender*	0	0	0	0	0	0
9	25	34	52	93	11	43
All commodities Unadjusted average	63	57	50	59	37	53
Adjusted average	65	60	53	63	39	56

* These numbers are 2-digit statistics in the 1963 Classification; the descriptions match different 2-digit statistics in the 1959 Classification.

TABLE A9.4
*Share of Intra-Industry Trade in Total Trade
Among EEC Countries, 1954*

SITC Classes	Belgium–Luxembourg	Netherlands	Germany	France	Italy	Mean
00	80	20	2	28	0	26
01	92	20	9	79	42	48
02	18	3	8	38	31	20
03	27	19	47	68	4	33
04	57	47	8	8	50	34
05	75	39	13	86	13	45
06	91	44	86	20	24	53
07	48	18	41	59	80	49
08	59	87	96	39	97	76
09	46	42	45	37	25	39
0	54	26	16	50	21	33
11	13	73	34	19	20	32
12	41	70	4	6	78	40
1	20	71	20	17	44	34
21	90	97	14	51	84	67
22	95	40	14	55	88	58
23	86	17	37	80	75	59
24	50	7	19	60	3	28
25	19	49	28	6	7	22
26	99	93	62	53	65	74
27	61	50	86	92	95	77
28	26	86	35	23	23	39
29	97	29	34	90	67	63
2	68	49	39	48	37	48
3	99	78	33	85	96	78
4	68	33	36	47	11	39
51	98	68	38	96	74	75
52	48	88	73	50	86	69
53	55	64	36	55	37	49
54	64	99	71	69	50	71
55	63	93	97	56	87	79
56	74	0	26	59	65	45
57 58 59	}84	89	45	99	65	76
5	79	70	43	82	66	68

SITC Classes	Belgium–Luxembourg	Netherlands	Germany	France	Italy	Mean
61	99	33	93	22	73	64
62	100	69	20	64	43	59
63	45	40	87	64	96	66
64	59	74	75	91	28	65
65	61	84	96	33	50	65
66	68	42	34	91	27	52
67	56	63	70	90	54	67
68	29	63	95	62	23	54
69	94	37	13	98	72	63
6	49	65	80	58	42	59
71	52	41	21	59	55	46
72	76	92	21	95	71	71
73	76	76	10	55	25	48
7	65	69	18	64	52	54
81	57	96	19	65	15	50
82	17	55	20	83	84	52
83	19	89	8	100	100	63
84	95	96	85	58	25	72
85	39	65	86	52	25	53
86	99	71	38	84	27	64
89	63	97	40	91	56	69
8	76	88	47	83	41	67
9	15	42	26	3	40	25
All commodities Unadjusted average	62	59	40	61	45	53
Adjusted average	64	62	51	73	52	60

Notes on Tables A9.1 to 9.4

1 These measures show the percentage of the trade of each member with the other five members *combined* in the commodities of the 2-digit division of the SITC, and of the totals for all divisions, which is intra-industry trade.

2 It was necessary to compute these measures of intra-industry trade at the 2-digit level of trade statistics because no 3-digit trade statistics are available from these sources for 1954. Furthermore, the total imports and exports of 3-digit commodities for these countries are not broken down into trade with individual countries in 1959, nor for some commodities in 1964 also.

3 At the 2-digit level the differences in the 1950 SITC classification used for 1954 and 1959 and the 1963 (rev.) SITC classification used for 1964 and 1967 are insignificant.

4 In the 1959 statistics the exports and imports of a few of the 3-digit commodities which were aggregated to form the 2-digit divisions are not broken down by individual countries. The omission of these flows from the statistics of global intra-industry does not bias the statistics significantly, as trade in these commodities was small.

5 There are two sources of error in the 1954 statistics. First, statistics of the 2-digit trade of the five countries are available only for the trade with 'Continental member countries' combined rather than the other EEC countries. In addition to the other EEC member countries, the group 'Continental member countries' includes Austria, Denmark, Greece, Norway, Portugal, Sweden, Switzerland, Trieste and Turkey. Secondly, no 2-digit statistics are available for Sections 3, 4 or 9, and the 1-digit statistics were used. Both these errors bias upwards the measures of global intra-industry trade among the EEC countries for this year compared with the three later sample years.

References

Adam, G., 'New Trends in International Business: Worldwide Sourcing and Dedomiciling', *Acta Oeconomica*, 7, 3–4 (1971) 349–71.

Adler, M., 'Specialisation in the European Coal and Steel Community', *Journal of Common Market Studies*, VII (March 1970) 175–91.

Atkinson, A. B. and Stiglitz, J. E., 'A New View of Technological Change', *Economic Journal*, 79, 315 (September 1969).

Balassa, B., 'An Empirical Demonstration of Classical Comparative Cost Theory', *Review of Economics and Statistics*, 45 (August 1963) 231–8.

—— 'Tariff Reductions and Trade in Manufactures among the Industrial Countries', *American Economic Review*, LVI (June 1966) 466–73.

—— *Trade Liberalization among Industrial Countries* (New York: McGraw-Hill, 1967).

Baldwin, R. E., 'The Commodity Composition of Trade; Selected Industrial Countries, 1950–54', *Review of Economics and Statistics*, XL (February 1958, Supplement) 51–68.

—— 'Determinants of the Commodity Structure of U.S. Trade', *American Economic Review*, LXI (March 1971) 126–46.

Baranson, J., *Automotive Industries in Developing Countries* (Baltimore: Johns Hopkins Press, 1969).

—— *International Transfer of Automotive Technology to Developing Countries*, United Nations Institute for Training and Research Reports, 8 (New York, 1971).

Bhagwati, J. N., 'Comment' in *The Technology Factor in International Trade*, ed. R. Vernon (New York: National Bureau of Economic Research, 1970).

—— and P. Desai, *India: Planning for Industrialization* (London: Oxford University Press, 1970).

194   *References*

Bradshaw, M. T., 'US Exports to Foreign Affiliates of US Firms', *Survey of Current Business*, 49 (May 1969) 34–51.

Bright, J. R., *Research Development and Technological Innovation: an Introduction* (Homewood, Ill.: Irwin, 1964).

Caves, R., *Trade and Economic Structure: Models and Methods* (Cambridge, Mass.: Harvard University Press, 1960).

—— 'International Corporations: The Industrial Economics of Foreign Investment', *Economica*, 38 (February 1971) 1–27.

Chipman, J. S., 'A Survey of the Theory of International Trade: Part 2, The Neo-Classical Theory', *Econometrica*, 33 (October 1965) 685–760.

Coase, R. H., "The Problem of Social Cost', *Journal of Law and Economics* (October 1966) 1–44.

Comanor, W. S. and H. Leibenstein, 'Allocative Efficiency, X-Efficiency, and the Measurement of Welfare Losses', *Economica*, XXXVI (1969) 304–9.

Commonwealth of Australia, Commonwealth Bureau of Census and Statistics, *Australian Exports, 1967–68*, Bulletin 10 (Canberra: Commonwealth Government Printing Office, 1969).

——, Tariff Board, *Tariff Board's Report on Hollow Bars, Tubes, and Pipes of Iron and Steel* (Canberra: Commonwealth Government Printing Office, 1965).

——, ——, *Annual Report for 1969–70* (Canberra: Commonwealth Government Printing Office, 1970).

Corden, W. M., 'Comment', in *Studies in International Economics*, eds. I. A. McDougall and R. H. Snape (Amsterdam: North-Holland, 1970).

——, *The Theory of Protection* (Oxford: Clarendon Press, 1971).

Daly, D. J., B. A. Keys and E. J. Spence, *Scale and Specialization in Canadian Manufacturing*, Staff Study 21 (Ottawa: Economic Council of Canada, 1968).

Dennison, E. F., *The Sources of Economic Growth* (Washington: Committee for Economic Development, 1962).

Drèze, J., 'Quelques Réflexions sereins sur l'adaptation de l'industrie belge au Marché Commun', *Comptes Rendues des Travaux de la Société Royale d'Economie Politique de Belgique*, 275 (December 1960).

——, 'Les Exportations intra-CEE en 1958 et la position belge', *Recherches Economiques de Louvain*, XXVII (1961) 717–38.

Drysdale, P., 'Japan, Australia, New Zealand: The Prospect for Western Pacific Economic Integration', *Economic Record*, 45 (September 1969) 321–42.

Frankel, H., 'Industrialisation of Agricultural Countries and the Possibilities of a New International Division of Labour, *Economic Journal*, 53 (June–September 1943) 188–201.

Gregory, R. G., 'U.S. Imports and Internal Pressure of Demand', *American Economic Review* (March 1971) 28–47.

—— and D. Tearle, 'Product Differentiation and International Trade Flows', *Australian Economic Papers*, 12 (June 1973) 79–90.

Griliches, Z. *et al.*, 'The Costs of Automobile Model Changes Since 1949', *Journal of Political Economy* (October 1962) 433–51.

Grubel, H. G., 'Intra-Industry Specialization and the Pattern of Trade', *Canadian Journal of Economics and Political Science*, XXXIII (August 1967) 374–88.

——, 'The Theory of Intra-Industry Trade', in *Studies of International Economics*, eds. I. A. McDougall and R. H. Snape (Amsterdam: North-Holland 1970).

—— and P. J. Lloyd, 'The Empirical Measurement of Intra-Industry Trade', *Economic Record*, 47 (December 1971) 494–517.

Helleiner, G., 'Manufactured Exports from Less Developed Countries and Multinational Firms', *Economic Journal*, LXXXIV (March 1973) 21–47.

Herberg, H. and M. C. Kemp, 'Some Implications of Variable Returns to Scale', *Canadian Journal of Economics*, 2 (August 1969) 403–15.

Hesketh, B., 'Intra-Industry Trade Specialisation in South-East Asia', unpublished M.A. thesis (Canberra: Australian National University) 1973.

Hilgerdt, F., 'The Approach to Bilateralism – A Change in the Structure of World Trade', *Svenska Mandelsbank Index* (August 1935) 175–88.

——, 'The Case for Multilateral Trade', *American Economic Review*, XXXIII (March 1943, Supplement) 393–407.

Hirsch, S., *Location of Industry and International Competitiveness* (Oxford: Clarendon Press, 1967).

Hirschman, A. O., *National Power and the Structure of Foreign Trade* (Berkeley and Los Angeles: University of California Press, 1945).

Houthakker, H. and S. Magee, 'Income and Price Elasticities in World Trade', *Review of Economics and Statistics* (May 1969) 111–25.

Hufbauer, G. C., *Synthetic Materials and the Theory of International Trade* (London: Duckworth, 1966).

——, 'The Impact of National Characteristics and Technology on Commodity Composition of Trade in Manufactured Goods', in *The Technology Factor in International Trade*, ed. R. Vernon (New York: National Bureau of Economic Research, 1970).

——, 'Specialization by Industrial Countries: Extent and Consequences', *Weltwirtschaftliches Archiv* (forthcoming).

Hunter, A., *Petroleum Prices in Australia. A Report to the Australian Automobile Association* (Canberra: Australian Automobile Association, 1969).

Janssen, L. H., *Free Trade, Protection and Customs Union* (Leiden: Stenfert Kroese, 1961).

Johnson, H. G., 'The Gains from Free Trade with Europe', *The Manchester School of Economic and Social Studies*, 26 (September 1958) 247–55.

——, 'International Trade Theory and Monopolistic Competition Theory', in *Monopolistic Theory: Studies in Impact*, ed. R. E. Kuenne (New York: John Wiley and Sons, 1967).

——, 'Comparative Cost and Commercial Policy for a Developing World Economy', Wicksell Lectures of 1968 (Stockholm: Almquist and Miksell, 1968).

——, 'The State of Theory in Relation to the Empirical Analysis', in *The Technology Factor in International Trade*, ed. R. Vernon (New York: National Bureau of Economic Research, 1970a).

——, 'The Efficiency and Welfare Implication of the International Corporation', in *The International Corporation*, ed. C. P. Kindleberger (Boston: MIT Press, 1970b).

Keesing, D. B., 'Labor Skills and International Trade: Evaluating Many Trade Flows with a Single Measuring Device',

Review of Economics and Statistics, 47 (August 1965) 287–94.

——, 'Labor Skills and Comparative Advantage', *American Economic Review*, LVI (May 1966) 249–58.

——, 'Comment', in *The Technology Factor in International Trade*, ed. R. Vernon (New York: National Bureau of Economic Research, 1970).

Kemp, M. C., *The Pure Theory of International Trade and Investment* (Englewood Cliffs: Prentice-Hall, 1969).

Kindleberger, C. P., *International Economics*, 4th ed. (Homewood, Ill.: Irwin, 1968).

——, *American Business Abroad* (New Haven: Yale University Press, 1969).

Kojima, K. (ed.), *Pacific Trade and Development*, Papers and Proceedings of a Conference held by the Japan Economic Research Center (The Japan Economic Research Center, February 1968).

Kojima, K., 'The Pattern of Triangular Trade among the U.S.A., Japan and South-East Asia', *The Developing Economics* (March–August 1962) 48–74.

——, 'The Pattern of International Trade among Advanced Countries', *Hitotsubashi Journal of Economics*, 5 (June 1964) 16–36.

——, *Japan and a Pacific Free Trade Area* (London: Macmillan, 1971).

Krause, L. B., 'European Economic Integration and the United States', *American Economic Review*, LIII (May 1963a) 185–96.

——, 'The European Economic Community and the United States Balance of Payments', in *The United States Balance of Payments in 1968*, ed. W. S. Salant (Washington: The Bookings Institution, 1963b).

Krauss, M. B., 'Recent Developments in Customs Union Theory: An Interpretive Survey', *Journal of Economic Literature*, X (June 1972) 413–36.

Kravis, I. B. and R. E. Lipsey, *Price Competitiveness in World Trade* (New York: National Bureau of Economic Research, 1971).

Lancaster, K., 'A New Approach to Consumer Theory', *Journal of Political Economy* (1966) 132–57.

League of Nations, *Review of World Trade, 1933* (Geneva, 1934).

——, *Review of World Trade, 1934* (Geneva, 1935).

——, *Review of World Trade, 1935* (Geneva, 1936).

——, *Review of World Trade, 1936* (Geneva, 1937).

——, *The Network of World Trade* (Geneva, 1942).

Leamer, E. E. and R. M. Stern, *Quantitative International Economics* (Boston: Allyn and Bacon, 1970).

Leibenstein, H., 'Allocative vs "X-Efficiency" ', *American Economic Review*, LVI (June 1966) 392–415.

Leontiades, J., 'International Sourcing in the LDC's', *Columbia Journal of World Business*, VI (September–October 1971) 24–30.

Levitt, K., *Silent Surrender: The Multinational Corporation in Canada* (Toronto: Macmillan, 1970).

Linder, S. B., *An Essay on Trade and Transformation* (New York: John Wiley and Sons, 1961).

Linneman, H., *An Econometric Study of International Trade Flows* (Amsterdam: North-Holland, 1966).

Little, I. M. D., 'Direct versus Indirect Taxes', *Economic Journal*, 61 (September 1951) 577–84.

Lloyd, P. J., *New Zealand Manufacturing Production and Trade with Australia*, New Zealand Institute of Economic Research, Research Paper 17 (Wellington: New Zealand Institute of Economic Research, 1971).

MacDougall, G. D. A., 'British and American Exports: A Study Suggested by the Theory of Comparative Costs', *Economic Journal*, LXI (December 1951) 697–724.

Maizels, A., *Industrial Growth and World Trade* (Cambridge University Press, 1963).

Major, R. L., 'The Common Market: Production and Trade', *National Institute Economic Review*, 21 (August 1962) 24–36.

Marshall, Alfred, *Industry and Trade* (London: Macmillan, 1919).

Mathews, R., *Industrial Viability in a Free Trade Economy: A Program of Adjustment Policies for Canada* (University of Toronto Press, 1971).

Michaely, M., *Concentration in International Trade* (Amsterdam: North-Holland, 1962a).

——, 'Multilateral Balancing in International Trade', *American Economic Review*, LII (September 1962b) 685–702.

Posner, M. V., 'International Trade and Technical Change', *Oxford Economic Papers*, 13 (October 1961) 323–41.

Rogers, E. M., *Diffusion of Innovations* (New York: Free Press, 1962).

Schumpeter, J., *Capitalism, Socialism and Democracy* (New York: Harper, 1942).

Scitovsky, T., *Economic Theory and West European Integration* (London: Allen and Unwin, 1958).

Servan-Schreiber, J. J., *The American Challenge* (New York: Avon Books, 1969).

Smith, V., *Investment and Production* (Cambridge, Mass.: Harvard University Press, 1961).

Verdoorn, P. J., 'The Intra-Bloc Trade of Benelux', in *Economic Consequences of the Size of Nations*, ed. E. A. G. Robinson (London: Macmillan, 1960).

Vernon, R. (ed.), *The Technology Factor in International Trade* (New York: National Bureau of Economic Research, 1970).

Vernon, R., 'International Investment and International Trade in the Product Cycle', *Quarterly Journal of Economics*, 80 (May 1966) 190–207.

Vukasovich, B., 'Intra-Industry Trade Rates: Yugoslavia and the Rest of the World', unpublished M.A. thesis (Wharton School, University of Pennsylvania, 1970).

Watkins, M. *et al.*, *Foreign Ownership and the Structure of Canadian Industry*, Report of the Trade Force on the Structure of Canadian Industry (Ottawa: Privy Council Office, 1968).

Willmore, L. N., 'Free Trade in Manufactures among Developing Countries: The Central American Experience', *Journal of Economic Development and Cultural Change*, 20, 4 (July 1972).

Wonnacott, R. J. and P. Wonnacott, *Free Trade between the United States and Canada* (Cambridge, Mass.: Harvard University Press, 1967).

Index